Deaccessioning Today

Deaccessioning Today

Theory and Practice

Steven Miller

ROWMAN & LITTLEFIELD
Lanham • Boulder • New York • London

Published by Rowman & Littlefield
A wholly owned subsidary of The Rowman & Littlefield Publishing Group, Inc.
4501 Forbes Boulevard, Suite 200, Lanham, Maryland 20706
www.rowman.com

Unit A, Whitacre Mews, 26–34 Stannary Street, London SE11 4AB

British Library Cataloguing in Publication Information Available

Library of Congress Cataloging-in-Publication Data

Names: Miller, Steven, 1947 - author.
Title: Deaccessioning today : theory and practice / Steven Miller.
Description: Lanham, Maryland : Rowman & Littlefield, 2018. | Includes
    bibliographical references and index.
Identifiers: LCCN 2017060131 (print) | LCCN 2017060289 (ebook) | ISBN
    9781538112649 (Electronic) | ISBN 9781538112625 (cloth : alk. paper) | ISBN
    9781538112632 (pbk. : alk. paper)
Subjects: LCSH: Museums—Collection management. | Museums—Deaccessioning.
Classification: LCC AM133 (ebook) | LCC AM133 .M55 2018 (print) | DDC
    069/.068—dc23
LC record available at https://lccn.loc.gov/2017060131

♾ ™ The paper used in this publication meets the minimum requirements of
American National Standard for Information Sciences—Permanence of Paper for
Printed Library Materials, ANSI/NISO Z39.48-1992.

Printed in the United States of America

To my fabulous family always,
with all my love always.
Dad

CONTENTS

LIST OF ILLUSTRATIONS

PREFACE

D*eaccessioning Today: Theory and Practice* explains why and how museums remove objects from their permanent collections. Traditionally this rarely happened, at least not in any official and organized way. Regardless of reasons for collection disposals, for the most part the public was unaware of such activities. Times have changed. The removal of items from a museum's permanent holdings is now a recognized and generally accepted practice within the greater museum field. Called *deaccessioning*, it is a viable collection management option.

While most museum collections are not candidates for removal, when they are the procedure must occur in a logical fashion following generally accepted professional guidelines. That process and those guidelines have been carefully fashioned over the past few decades. They are referenced in this text through both a narrative and workbook perspective.

There are many reasons for deaccessioning, and these must be completely understood by museums. Most of the time this action happens without incident. However, on occasion it can be extremely controversial.

Because museums are defined by their collections, how these are treated is of obvious concern. That concern embraces exhibition, conservation, scholarship, acquisition, and, on occasion, deaccessioning. *Deaccessioning Today: Theory and Practice* explains the range of considerations about why museums delete objects from their collections. It presents ways of doing so, including how to explain the action publicly. And it touches on controversies that can erupt on occasion. Sample deaccession actions are briefly discussed, and suggested best practices are listed.

Deaccessioning Today is written for the museum field as well as those interested in that world. Readers will include staff, trustees, funders, cultural lawmakers, and those already involved in the profession. It will be of special relevance for museum studies students. The topic is of immense importance for museums now. The book avoids strong opinions about deaccessioning and offers a neutral overview of the subject.

The scope of *Deaccessioning Today* is comprehensive while avoiding murky or extraneous verbiage. It is organized in a linear and practical manner reflecting current realities and profession guidelines. The goal is to be understood by experienced museum employees as well as those with little or no knowledge of that field. The approach is to provide simple but complete coverage for a subject of central importance to museum collection management now. There is no single book on the topic that is as inclusive, comprehensive, and succinct. Two books have been previously published about deaccessioning, but they are compendiums of opinion essays. In that capacity they reflect a more scattered approach to the topic.

The topic of deaccessioning has been written about extensively in the press, discussed in museum profession workshops, lectures, and other presentations, and it is now included in most museum policies and operations manuals. Articles have been written for trade publications. However, there is no single book that addresses it in a helpful, comprehensive, condensed manner. There is no comprehensive list of why museums remove items from permanent collections. There is no broad overview of the options museums have for implementing a deaccession. There is no book that provides a philosophical background on museums in the context of collections and deaccessioning. This book attempts to fill those voids.

Deaccessioning Today aims to give people a way of understanding deaccessioning, why and how it can and might be implemented, and what pitfalls to watch for before, during, and after the process. The content of the book can be used as a checklist for discussions and applications.

I have written and lectured extensively about deaccessioning since the early 1970s. Writings have appeared in the United States and abroad and in museum policies. In addition, I have participated in panel discussions, workshops, and other presentations for the museum field. As a museum curator and director with several decades of experience regarding collection management, I have instituted deaccessions for a wide variety of objects. The topic is a specialty, but one that continues to unfold and change.

Deaccessioning Today is organized in a straightforward manner. The first chapter discusses what museums are, their origins, and how they operate. The second chapter addresses the central role collections play and provides background information about what deaccessioning is and how it has emerged as an important topic for museums. This notion is essential when it comes to removing objects. The third chapter explains why deaccessioning happens. It lists twenty reasons for the action. These can be promulgated by museums or forced on them. Because the practice can be so idiosyncratic, decisions range from the obvious to the peculiar, the commonly acceptable to the suspect. Chapter 4 explains museum-initiated deaccessions and those forced on museums. Chapter 5 reviews implementation options for museums. Because deaccessioning can on occasion be controversial, chapter 6 discusses why this happens and how museums may or may not want to contribute to or respond to debates; this chapter concludes with final thoughts about deaccessioning. Six appendices round out the book, covering deaccessioning policies, example press releases, and a sample deaccession list.

ACKNOWLEDGMENTS

I would like to acknowledge four people who were incredibly important mentors during the early years of my career: Albert K. Baragwanath (senior curator, Museum of the City of New York), Joseph Veach Noble (director, Museum of the City of New York), Louis Auchincloss (board chair, Museum of the City of New York), and Paul Rivard (director, Maine State Museum). I owe them a debt of eternal gratitude. I would like to thank Sandy Wood for her superior editing of my quixotic manuscript.

AN INTRODUCTION TO MUSEUMS

Museums as we know them now are recent inventions. As currently configured, they are only a few hundred years old. Of course, people have been collecting historic relics, art, and natural science specimens since Homo sapiens started walking upright . . . if not before. Ancient cave art proves this, as do Classical Roman private collections of Greek sculpture as well as art made for or incorporated into places of worship. Ancient burial sites, religious reliquaries, and thousands of churches in Christendom offer prime examples too.

Clearly people have a deep-rooted psychological connectivity for individually or group-designated physical evidence with self-generated values for art, history, or the natural world. The collecting practices of most museums as they developed over the past several centuries had the goal in mind of the long-range retention for objects of veneration, intellectual content, or important visual meaning. This preservation idea was and remains verbally expressed by museum creators, sustainers, expanders, and changers. It is always explained in the concept of benefiting a, or the general, public. These defining characteristics remain in effect today.

The wisdom or foolishness of museums as we know them are matters of personal preference, opinion, interest, and life pursuits. It is probably safe to say most people rarely if ever visit museums. Yet for whatever reasons, since their establishment they have proliferated, albeit some strongly and some weakly.

Today there are museums of all kinds all over the world, and they continue to be formed. At their core, they are celebratory in nature, and even overly proselyze. They were started with a lofty, socially beneficial mission in mind. Whether or not that mission was appealing to the many or the few was almost immaterial. Those manifesting a museum believed in its "cause," "purpose," brand," "idea," "value," and more. In application the meaning of a museum was realized by getting, studying, and explaining objects that in time formed collections of relevance. As museums matured the concept was to hold these items in perpetuity.

Once owned by museums, collections pretty much remained intact. Rarely were they removed, and when that happened it was often the consequence of an unfortunate event such as war, natural disaster, or theft. Recently, however, the idea that things can be deleted by museums, of their own volition, for operational reasons has become accepted within the museum profession as a legitimate collection management option. Extensive discussions, debates, and conversations have taken place both on a formal and informal level to explain how, why, and when collections can and are reduced. The practice is known as *deaccessioning*.

This book offers a practical outline about deaccessions as it currently happens. A brief historical overview of museums is included, but the focus is on present circumstances. The purpose is to be helpful and provide guidance within the museum field. It is important for those in governing authority over museums as, in the end, they will usually make the final official decision about why something leaves museum ownership. The book can also have informative applications for people otherwise interested in museums, how they operate, and why. These will presumably include members of the media, museum donors, government agencies that fund museums, and foundations that provide support for these unique institutions.

Brief History of Museums

Today, around the globe there are at least several million museums investigating, interpreting, and celebrating art, science, and history interests. Whether ordinary, odd, or unique, these institutions have gone well beyond their Eurocentric origins. They can range from small all-volunteer operations with tiny budgets to large institutions with significant financial resources and scores of paid staff who specialize in everything from maintenance to security to curating to directing. Museums are found in rural areas, small towns, suburbs, and big cities. Many have been in existence for decades and even centuries. Some are brand new. Indeed, museums continue to be formed with astonishing frequency.

Museums are founded and run by individuals. They can be independent legal entities, part of businesses, or owned and operated by larger parent organizations. They may belong to governments. The vast majority of museums own, collect, and use objects to meet their end purposes. It is important to understand that regardless of type, museums tend to function in similar ways. How things are obtained, cared for, used, and presented to viewers follows certain accepted museum operational practices and protocols. Yet though they might appear to be rife with committees, personal influence is the norm.

The museum as we know it is a child of the Enlightenment and the great Age of European Exploration. The phenomenon of a nonreligious repository of things gotten and held indefinitely for some shared civic and often celebratory good began to robustly manifest itself in organized ways in the eighteenth century. The concept placed the public (however that might be defined) as ultimate beneficiaries. Historic examples include the Louvre (1793), Paris; the Kuntskamera (1727), Saint Petersburg, Russia; the Charleston Museum (1773), Charleston, South Carolina; the Rijksmuseum (1800), Amsterdam; and the British Museum (1753), London, to name a very few. Evolutionary precursors to museums were evidenced in at least three existing forms. There was art found in government buildings and churches, religious reliquaries purportedly held physical evidence of meaning, and "cabinets of curiosities" assembled by the wealthy featured natural history specimens as well as "oddities" brought back from excursions to "exotic" lands far beyond European environs.

As commonplace as government, religious, or personal assemblages of stuff might have been, they fell far short of what was crystalized institutionally in the eighteenth century as the core template of today's museum. That notion centers on forming collections of things for a valued purpose beyond private ruling power or ecclesiastical applications. As they were invented and evolved over the past three to four hundred years, museums defined themselves as places that acquired, studied, kept, and presented physical materials for reasons of some shared benefit or purpose. That benefit and purpose could be for political, cultural, social, economic, or academic desires, or combinations thereof. To be sure, museums have never been neutral places absent doctrinal perspectives, but they have set these perspectives presumably for lofty educational reasons even if reflecting opinionate views. We see this in the proliferation of museums devoted to specialized subjects honoring topics, people, places, events, ideas, and more.

The nineteenth century witnessed the founding of thousands of museums across Europe and in hemispheres touched by the European diaspora. These decades saw the fledgling concept of a museum become a viable and worthy cultural reality. The premise of these entities rested on the concept that certain objects are worth being acquired, studied, and held in public trust for the evidence they provide to prove informational, cultural, and emotional value. Institutionalizing that notion, which is what museums do for whatever reason, resulted in the establishment of so-called permanent collections. Thus, over time, museums became cohesive repositories for what today are vast holdings of things relating to all manner of subjects. Indeed, name a topic and the chances are good that physical evidence of it will be found in a museum or museums somewhere. Regardless of why a museum exists, it is the collecting and the collections that give it meaning, purpose, and identity.

An essential requirement for starting and sustaining museums was at least a modicum of regular social stability. Museums often suffer terribly during times of political unrest and catastrophic violence. Though upheavals of all sorts were common in Europe when the modern museum was being born, enough periods and places of calm existed for the concept to take root and become an accepted societal reality.

Almost from the time of their invention, museums defined and divided themselves according to three scholarly disciplines. The divisions continue to this day. They are subject focused and cover science, art, and history. The topics reflect established intellectual occupations as well as founding preferences. Artists and those interested in art were inclined to organize art museums. Scientists had obvious shared academic concerns, especially relating to the natural universe. History buffs wanted places (shrines?) devoted to some aspect or aspects of the human past. A few museums combined these interests, notably anthropology, archaeology, and, since the 1960s, children's museums.

Certain overarching governmental agencies or private entities may be responsible for a mix of museums representing the aforementioned three typologies. The Smithsonian Institution in Washington, DC, might appear in theory to be an amalgam of museums, but in practice it follows a traditional museum separation pattern. It has the Smithsonian American Art Museum, the National Museum of American History, and the National Museum of Natural History. There are other branches and operative parts, but the customary divisions of the museum mindset are apparent to the general public.

An enhanced social focus, diverse ownership arrangements, or increasing attendance numbers have not altered the centrality of the object when it comes to what most museums do, why and how. In fact, it has only intensified the core role collections play as primary documents used to help cipher and decipher meanings. This is apparent when new museums form and relevant collections are sought. The new Museum of African American History and Culture, on the Mall in Washington, DC, offers an excellent example. When it was being planned, enormous energy went into seeking and acquiring a huge array of objects of immediate and obvious relevance to the experience—positive or negative—of African Americans in this country. We see shifts in collecting priorities when museums need to present art or artifacts relating to aspects of their subject that are newly prominent in either intellectual or public circles. The importance of art and artifacts is especially obvious in the dramatic rise of repatriation claims made by a host of cultures who feel their tangible patrimony was wrongly taken from them in the distant past. These actions can grow out of political, social, demographic, or economic motivations or combinations thereof. Usually (one hopes) the things being sought will join the permanent collections of museums in the places from whence the objects came. These international discussions and debates reflect the idea that museums themselves are political, social, demographic, or economic acts.

Science museums provide intriguing examples of the importance of often odd sorts of collections. These fundamentally research-based institutions rely on vast holdings of flora and fauna specimens to cause and create theories, provide proof, and allow for substantive scholarship and academic investigations. Staff are daily engaged with diverse objects, from rocks and minerals to bugs and bones to birds and flowers.

Museum Collections

Collection value (nonmonetary) depends on collection content. This requires knowing an object's informational status and potential. From inception, determining intrinsic or associated meanings for things was and remains the key job museums assigned themselves. It is what makes them unique. For whatever reason, the public accepts and expects this institutionally declared purpose. Consequently, to properly and best fulfill their missions, museums must collect objects in some deliberative and intellectually cogent manner with a relevant objective in mind. That goal, which in application can vary over time, calls for objects to be seen (literally) as conduits substantiating meaningful aspects of the human experience and natural world.

Museum collections are central to explicating knowledge. Yet they are far more than just convenient image sources for books, PowerPoint talks, or online conversations. Museums are communication centers. Through their collections they communicate with past, present, and we hope, future generations. Today the tangible links us to the intangible. Stuff, objects, the physical, and more are connective talismans to, about, and for ideas, concepts, meanings, feelings, and thinking. Things link us to people, places, and events. How they do so and to what effect varies.

For museums to espouse the meaning of objects, certain employees are designated to decide what objects should be obtained and saved in perpetuity. These people usually hold the title of curator. The job implies, requires, and is expected to reflect a knowledge about the sort of material culture pertinent to a museum's mission. This deliberative process results in collecting.

When a museum starts there might be a less disciplined approach to filling galleries and storage areas. This was especially true in the past. Museums have always abhorred spatial vacuums. Empty rooms are not empty for long. Gradually, as museums define and refine themselves by the collections they own, an acquisition and retention logic unfolds. That logic can be obvious or odd. A museum of American art will presumably collect art about or of America and by Americans. But there may be peculiar inclusions because ways of explaining America and what is American ebbs and flows. Philosophies of collecting (especially if object storage is full or overflowing) are leading to a more rigorous contemplation about what museums own and why. To a degree this is a positive development.

The idea that museums collect, ceaselessly, is embedded in their psyche. The public believes it is what these places do. Globally, quadrillions of objects reside within museums. However, in the past few decades, especially in the United States, questions have arisen about whether everything an institution owns deserves to be there, or should even be retained regardless of mission relevancy. Consequently, analytical retention inquiries are now a component of a professional museum operation. Collection assessment is a ceaseless stewardship duty.

Most museum collections are usually appropriate for most museums and will stay put for quite some time. Yet not every object may be needed. Acquisition errors or miscalculations have and do occur. They will continue to occur, albeit less frequently as the museum profession matures regarding the idea that each and every item in a collection must have a clear and obvious role as an explicator.

Deaccessioning

Reviewing museum collections for relevance, content, and condition is an increasingly common and recommended practice. The result of such exercises can cause items to be removed from museum collections. Occasionally a museum may even decide it is no longer interested in whole aspects of a subject, and entire collections related to that topic become candidates for departure.

It is the nature of museums to be acquisitive. This act is regularly heralded to the public when new acquisitions are announced or preservation projects promoted. The idea of jettisoning collections was once thought an exceptional, and even suspect, act. The assumption that museums only expanded and never contracted was always incorrect. But when deaccessioning, as it is now known, received widespread media attention in the United States in the early 1970s, it raised more than a few eyebrows (see chapter 6, Deaccession and Controversy, for a discussion on this topic). Controversy exploded, and it still can when collections are removed, regardless of how logical the reasons. What was an occasional collection management option became a practice fraught with potentially devastating public relations acrimony. As a result, guidelines, protective procedures, and suggested institutional and professional safeguards must be part of a collection removal process and outcome. For the most part, these are in place both on an institutional level and within broader professional perspectives.

Deaccessioning as discussed in this book reflects an American perspective. It is done in other countries, but the approaches, motivations, and consequences are often quite different. This reflects ownership differences between American museums and those in other nations. The vast majority of museums in the United States are privately owned and operated entities. The vast majority of museums outside the United States are government owned and operated. This means the collections they hold are "owned" by the citizens of a particular nation. The idea of disposing of this cultural patrimony ranges from impossible to peculiar to acceptable.

Deaccessioning: A Definition

The practice and process of removing accessioned museum collections is called deaccessioning, whether it results from an internally agreed upon and sanctioned institutional decision or is caused by forces beyond a museum's control.

For the purpose of this discussion, accessioned things are collection items that have been officially assigned and affixed with a unique numerical, alphanumerical, or similar inventory identification, usually as part of a cataloguing measure. An accession number can apply to a single object or a group of objects depending on a museum's customary practice and preference. Art museum collections are often made up of individual items and may be less prone to group numbering, while history museums find this a convenient way of accessioning things that have many component parts, such as a tea service set. Science museums, which for the purposes of this discussion will also include archeology and anthropology collections, can assign quite different numeral identities. Regardless of why or how it happens, any process of walking the accession act backward to officially relinquish an object from a museum collection can be construed as deaccessioning.

It must be noted that deaccessioning does not apply to things found in museums that were never accessioned. While similar safeguards and cautions may be recommended when dealing with these materials, they fall outside the official realm of the collection and collecting responsibilities museums assume for what has been formally acquired in an intentional and recorded manner. Operationally segregating accessioned and nonaccessioned things is no reflection on the value, importance, and desirability of objects without numbers. It is a definitional and procedure differentiation. Indeed, sometimes these orphans deserve to be accessioned.

How to deal with nonaccessioned things of "museum quality" that are in museums but are not accessioned is a subject requiring special consideration. Assessing the reasons why such things are present is a process of solving mysteries while deciding retention outcomes. If retention by inclusion in the museum collection is done, the item is accessioned. But if removal is the outcome, that is not deaccessioning.

Defining a Museum

Before examining deaccessioning at length, including how, why, and when it is done, there must be common agreement on what a museum is. Dictionaries are sufficient at providing rudimentary definitions of a general nature. However, when considering the centrality of permanent collections, more encompassing characteristics should be specified. Those usually reflect an idealistic institutional purpose.

A museum is a conceptual social construct invented to meet no pressing practical need. Consequently, the invention often has the liberty, or aspirations, to do whatever it wants, however it wants, whenever it wants. As with so many human concoctions, the museum as idea is the museum as reality. That transformation leads to a host of practical considerations that contrive to make museums operate in logical, obvious, productive, and cost-effective ways. Collecting is at the top of a museum's considerations. Though historically this activity might have been applied in a sometimes quixotic, idiosyncratic, and even illogical manner, approaches to collecting are now far more disciplined. This evolution has had an important influence on how museums are defined and why and how they acquire or remove collections.

In practice, a museum is essentially: *A public service preservation organization that explains subjects through objects. The objects hold verifiable evidential connections to and proof of the subjects being addressed.* There is an intellectual and actual reportorial transition that occurs when things enter museums. They are used to illustrate facts, theories, and ideas, as well as provide proof of and tell about places, people, and events. Deconstructing this construct shows why museum collections exist. They are relevant evidence.

Public service means providing something beneficial that people presumably want or like or need while making the act and fact of that service obvious and accessible. Though few actually need museums, given the survival rate and growth of them over the past three hundred years it would appear they are liked and wanted. Public service further suggests an endeavor reaching beyond the simple operations and outcomes of a commercial entity or private hobby. There is the altruistic notion of contributing to a common and shared good.

Museums recognize the concept of existing for and on behalf of the public, or at least *a* public. This is set forth in founding documents, mission statements, by-laws, and personnel policies and is regularly declared through media and other reporting conduits. The public service aspect of museums materializes in the host of activities, events, programs, publications, research, and more constantly unfolding in them. Ultimately, collections provide the grist supporting and proving official museum declarations and operations. Collecting, along with all the museological responsibilities it entails, is a public service.

Defining a museum's public is important for all aspects of an organization's mission and operation. It is especially critical when it comes to making deaccessioning decisions. If one defines a museum's public by who visits, there will actually be several publics. Most are there to see exhibits, but others are doing research, attending events, or conducting work of some sort. (Maintenance contractors, special event caterers, and commercial tour guides are some of the last category.) People looking at exhibitions can be subdivided into a range of "publics" including specialists in the topics of a particular exhibition, amateurs in that subject, the simply curious, those present because they were made to visit, and some who chanced upon an exhibition while doing something else. Notions about collection retention or loss will be far from their minds. If asked, the vast majority will affirm a common belief that what they see there will be around for the long term, though not necessarily on exhibit. Few will know or be concerned with the practice of deaccessioning.

The preservation duty that museums set for themselves plays out in their devotion to collections. To be sure, through their language museums also preserve whatever subject they embrace, but that is an abstract rather than concrete engagement. How it unfolds in practice will, of course, affect collections. Decisions regarding what to acquire, care for, and retain fluctuate according to existing or newly postulated spoken and written ideas about what is worth having and keeping at a particular institution.

No other human endeavor declares or even suggests assembling and holding inert physical evidence in perpetuity and doing a good job of it. While there is a certain hubris to this idea, it constitutes the museum playbook. The profession has designated operational components to achieve its stewardship goals. These include directing, curating, fundraising, education, exhibition, conservation, security, maintenance, and marketing.

As museum work has become a field of defined disciplines, organizing and being organized managerially and operationally at all levels is required and happens. This is especially apparent for institutional governance. No museum in America can or will survive for long unless it exists under the auspices of a body of people who hold a nonremunerative philanthropic responsibility for it. Such bodies are commonly referred to as boards of trustees. Even museums owned by governments have oversight volunteer appointees serving in monitoring and compliance capacities. These are found at national, regional, state, and local levels. The individuals who serve on museum boards are, ultimately, responsible for collections even if they are not knowledgeable about them. In fact, this is usually the case. Therefore, great care must be exercised when it comes to acquiring collections. Even greater care is necessary when removing collections.

The definition of a museum as a public service preservation organization that explains objects through subjects sets a conceptual armature for collecting, collection retention, and collection removals, depending on how or if the objects in question are "original" to the subject of a particular museum. Reproductions, copies, fakes, facsimiles, and more generally fall outside museum collection parameters (though there are exceptions). With that requirement in mind, questions are always asked in the arcane universe of museum scholarship. Is an object worth acquiring as a public service? If so, does the place acquiring it have the organizational capacity to preserve, study, and present it in effective and meaningful ways? As an integral part of an altruistic endeavor, can the object directly and obviously shed light on a subject? These are core considerations under discussion when acquiring museum collections. They must also be core considerations when removing collections.

CHAPTER TWO
DEACCESSIONING

Background

A merican museums tend to possess their collections free and clear of ownership encumbrances, restrictions, or caveats. Rarely are there any legal requirements about how they can be used, whether for exhibitions, research, storage, or removal. From their inception, museums generally had the good sense to avoid ownership entanglements when agreeing to accept something into their collections. This preference continues. There are exceptions to be sure, but they are just that. Usually they confirm the wisdom of eschewing proprietorial strings. Unfettered ownership permits maximal collection management.

Historical Issues with Deaccessioning

The vast majority of objects museums hold are kept with no intention of getting rid of them. However, this always needs to be an option. Actually, removing collections from museums is nothing new. A collection of Egyptian antiquities acquired by an English physician, Dr. Henry Abbott, in the second quarter of the nineteenth century and placed on view in New York City for the public to enjoy, offers an interesting example. When it was clear that Abbott's Egyptian Museum, or Egyptian Gallery, at 659 Broadway was for naught, the collection was purchased by the New-York Historical Society. Founded in 1804, the Society is one of the oldest museums in America. It had a somewhat broad mission when it bought the collection in 1860. Today it emphasizes New York City and American history. In 1937, the Society placed the collection on long-term loan to the Brooklyn Museum. The antiquities were much more appropriate for this encyclopedic international art museum. It bought the collection in 1948 and remains a core part of that institution's important Egyptian holdings (Maurita 2011).

In 1938, the Museum of Modern Art deaccessioned and sold a painting (*The Racecourse*) by Degas to help pay for the purchase of Picasso's 1907 revolutionary eight-foot square painting *Les Demoiselles d'Avignon* (Bee and Elligott 2004).

A profession has a language of its own, and the museum field is gradually developing one. Certainly it is not as arcane or obscure as might be found in the sciences, for instance, but it is evolving nevertheless. *Deaccessioning* is now part of the museum field's nomenclature. The term came to widespread public attention and common application in the 1970s when the Metropolitan Museum of Art was "caught" selling things from its collection. The practice was front-page news. The exposé was spearheaded by John Canaday, a *New York Times* cultural affairs reporter (Canaday 1972). Other journalists contributed. Heated debates erupted. They centered on why and how museum collection departures occurred (Hess 1974).

Because the media loves bringing to public attention things it considers questionable when done secretly by people in positions of power, and, because the Metropolitan Museum of Art was not initially forthcoming about its deaccessioning practices, reporters had a field day investigating the matter. Ironically, the more deaccessioning was discussed in both the media and museum circles the more the practice became accepted. Gradually the idea was recognized as a legitimate way to handle certain collection conundrums *if* certain museological protocols were articulated and put in place.

Deaccessioning Today

Today, deaccessioning is usually practiced without controversy. Nevertheless, museums are cautioned to tread carefully when jettisoning collections. Typically, complaints about the practice are (and historically were) generated outside the confines of museums. There are probably three reasons for this: when done in an appropriate manner, people in museums know or assume what is taking place is for legitimate reasons; few employees risk job security by contradicting decisions their employer makes; and colleagues prefer not to critique each other in public.

Setting aside past controversies surrounding deaccessioning, the practice is recognized as an acceptable collection management option. Guidelines have been established by the American Alliance of Museums (see the textbox below), the American Association for State and Local History, the Association of Art Museum Directors (see appendix I), and the International Council of Museums. Regional museum associations note it in membership materials. Excellent instructional chapters are contained in two important museum profession books: Marie C. Malaro and Ildiko

---

American Alliance of Museums Code of Ethics

Adopted 1991, amended 2000

Collections

- Acquisition, disposal, and loan activities are conducted in a manner that respects the protection and preservation of natural and cultural resources and discourages illicit trade in such materials.

- Acquisition, disposal, and loan activities confirm to its mission and public trust responsibilities.

- Disposal of collections through sale, trade, or research activities is solely for the advancement of a museum's mission. Proceeds from the sale of nonliving collections are to be used consistent with the established standards of the museum's discipline, but in no event shall they be used for anything other than acquisition or direct care of collections.

AAM members may also visit the AAM's website and refer to the Resource Library for more deaccession information.

Source: American Alliance of Museums, Code of Ethics for Museums (adopted 1991, amended 2000), http://aam-us.org/resources/ethics-standards-and-best-practices/code-of-ethics. Used with permission.

Pogany DeAngelis, *A Legal Primer for Managing Museum Collections*, 3rd edition (New York: Smithsonian Books, 2012), chapter V, "The Disposal of Objects, Deaccessioning," 248–72; and Rebecca A. Buck and Jean Allman Gilmore, *Museum Registration Methods*, section 3I, "Deaccessioning," Martha Morris, updated by Antonia Moser, 100–7 (American Alliance of Museums, 2010).

Deaccessioning is referenced in museum operating and governance policies. They list criteria for considering the removal of a collection item, suggest how it should be done, and note positive consequences for the museum. These usually focus on improvements for a museum's remaining collections. Benefits can include better storage conditions, direct conservation treatment to objects, and the ability to purchase new acquisitions.

Deaccessioning is done by museums across America. This is readily apparent when looking at scores of auction catalogues published by such major companies as Sotheby's and Christie's. Figure 2.1 shows a sampling of auction catalogues featuring deaccessioned collections. It is not unusual to see museum consigners listed as owners of various lots. Included will be a comment declaring that the sale was authorized by the institution's board of trustees and how the proceeds will be allocated. Sometimes even whole catalogues are devoted to one large deaccessioning project by a single museum. The ownership credit line is desirable for several reasons:

- It supports a museum's goal to be fully transparent when it comes to deaccessioning.

- It indicates what will be done with the proceeds.

- A history of museum ownership could attract a better sale price.

Most museums have the legal right to deaccession collections as and when they wish. However, a few are restricted from doing so. Others may have to abide by directives on how removals can happen. These caveats need to be contained in governance documents or are the result of laws. Museums must be aware of the presence or absence of actual or potential deaccession restrictions when contemplating deaccessioning.

The four most important deaccessioning questions to address are:

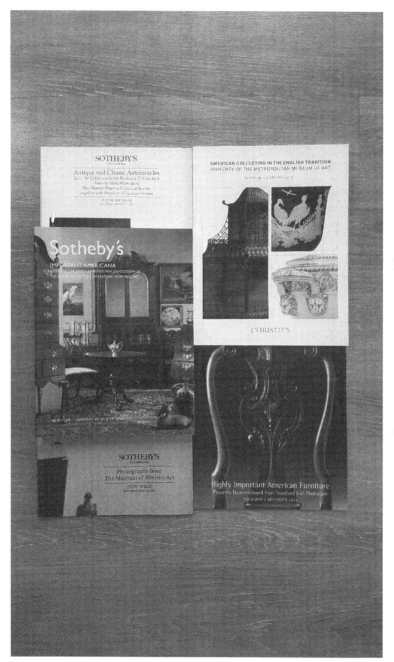

Figure 2.1. A sampling of auction catalogues featuring collections deaccessioned by museums. Photo by Steven Miller.

1. Why does a museum want to remove an object(s)?
2. Is the removal permissible?
3. What procedures can, will, should, or must be followed from start to finish?
4. If a sale is the allowed and preferred option, how will the income be used?

These questions may be separate, but they are also intertwined. Answers to one can often depend on answers to the others. They are listed in priority order, though that may not be how deaccessioning happens in the real world of a museum. For instance, sale may be the first and only reason a museum deaccessions something. Responding positively to one or all does not necessarily mean a deaccession is worth doing, but skipping one or more will almost certainly lead to problems.

When planning a deaccession policy, it is essential to list pertinent reasons to remove collections. These may be philosophical, practical, or political in nature, but all should be mission based. There can be one or several reasons for removing collections. These may depend on the nature of a particular museum, its governance structure, the scope and subject of its collections, potential and actual community sensitivities regarding the museum, and the legal status of the museum and the ownership of its collections. The following chapter lists commonly applied deaccession criteria for museums, be these acceptable or questionable in practice.

References

Bee, Harriet S., and Michelle Elligott, editors. 2004. *Art in Our Time: A Chronicle of the Museum of Modern Art*. New York: Museum of Modern Art.

Canaday, Joan. 1972. "Very Quiet and Very Dangerous." *New York Times*, February 27. http://www.nytimes.com/1972/02/27/archives/very-quiet-and-very-dangerous.html.

Hess, John L. 1974. *The Grand Acquisitors*. New York: Houghton Mifflin.

Maurita. 2011. "Egypt on Broadway." *From the Stacks. New-York Historical Society Museum Library* (blog). September 19, 2011. http://blog.nyhistory.org/egypt-on-broadway/.

REASONS FOR DEACCESSIONING

There are many reasons why museums deaccession collections. Some are obvious and logical. Others are obscure and even secret. Over the past few decades, it has become preferable and customary for museums to explain in some public manner why they are removing an object or objects. Published statements may be brief or lengthy, but any attempt at transparency is laudable.

Understanding arguments for deaccessioning reveals a museum's operating motivations, fiscal attitude, stewardship commitments, and employee and trustee interests as well as evolving practices surrounding the ownership of material culture for public benefit.

Museum conversations about removing collections vacillate. Debates can swirl around how wise or foolish, proper or irresponsible, shortsighted or overdue a deaccession might be. There may be strong preferences in favor of an action as well as harsh opinions against it. We hope those who make removal decisions about museum collections are qualified to do so. Presumably their actions accrue to the best interest of the museum and its collections as well as the public. Generally, this is the case. Sometimes it is not.

The people within museums who have the most influence when it comes to removing collections are trustees, directors, and curators. Donors (or heirs), if they are alive, may be included after the fact, but their impact is often negligible, random, or idiosyncratic. Rarely does the public have any involvement with deaccessions, unless a debate erupts that people feel strongly about. A similar absence of public participation happens with acquisitions. One stellar exception took place when citizens were invited by the Philadelphia Museum of Art and the Pennsylvania Academy of Fine Arts to help them share the purchase of Thomas Eakins's painting *The Gross Clinic* in 2007 (Vogel 2008).

Most deaccessioning is not questioned or questionable. To start with, the subject rarely involves more than a handful of people. It is hardly an action that unfolds with great fanfare in some open public forum. Bold media alerts are rare, though a media announcement may be issued. Reasons for deaccessioning are largely a matter of institutional opinion. The validity for removing something from a museum may be obvious or obscure. If it does not violate a law or laws, or contradict agreed-upon donor covenants or museum policies, deaccessioning usually proceeds without disruption. Yet on occasion it can be the subject of considerable public debate.

Museums deaccession collections for one or several of the following reasons. This list neither confirms the validity of a reason nor suggests a priority order.

- Mission Relevancy: An object is not pertinent to a museum's purpose.

- Retention Cost: The museum cannot afford to keep certain things.

- Storage Challenge: There is no storage space, or it is at such a premium that content needs to be reduced.

- Ignorance of an Item(s): There is no information or knowledge about a collection.

- Conservation is untenable.

- Ownership is in dispute.

- Collection Duplication: An item is a duplicate or triplicate of things in the collection.

- Redundancy: There are too many similar items in the collections.

- Fake or Forgery: Something is not original as once thought.

- Copies or Reproductions.

- Poor Quality.

- Exhibition Absence: Something has rarely or never been on view for the public.

- Source of Income: Collections can be sold for operating funds.

- Safety Threat: An item poses danger to other collections or to people.

- Appropriate for Another Museum.

- Unable to Meet Acquisition Restrictions.

- Stolen, Destroyed, or Missing Item.

- Violation of Conflict-of-Interest Policy.

- Unpopular Items: A trustee or trustees or an employee in authority doesn't like something.

- Combination of Reasons.

Mission Relevancy

When there is a hierarchy of reasons for deleting collections from a museum, mission irrelevancy is often at the top. Sometimes this is clear. A museum devoted to the history of New York City might gladly deaccession a deck chair it acquired years ago that is purportedly from the *Titanic* (which, while destined for New York City, sank before arriving).

It is essential to periodically assess what is in a museum's collections and why. Regular reviews of mission relevancy must be an operating necessity for assuring at least a modicum of collection logic. While the overarching mission of a museum may not change, how that mission is realized vis-à-vis a permanent collection is always subject to consideration and reconsideration.

Often there is an assumption that defining mission relevancy for collections can be easily and comprehensively spelled out in official documents such as by-laws, collection management policies, collecting plans, and more. Given the stupendous variety of things museums can reasonably acquire in the course of their work, it is almost impossible to write acquisition directives listing precisely what should be obtained and held.

Collecting is hardly a narrowly defined objective pursuit. Ultimately, it is entirely subjective and quite broad, even quixotic. But general parameters do need to be agreed upon and recorded, as previously cited. When well written, collection policies set critical parameters and also help museums decline inapplicable objects. The aforementioned New York City museum illustration offers a simple example. An obvious institutional collecting policy might deter a car museum from having a collection of sea shells, or a natural history museum having a collection of uniforms, or an American art museum having Peruvian ceramics. Some overarching control is necessary, regardless of how appealing nonrelevant items might be.

Periodically museums will dramatically change or appreciably alter a core mission or aspect thereof. An outcome of such adjustment will be the deaccessioning of collections that may not conform to the new or adjusted mission. The Albright-Knox Art Gallery in Buffalo, New York, did this in 2007. The board of trustees decided to focus exclusively on contemporary art. Collections that fell far outside this scope were sold at auction (see figure 3.1). The action was not without controversy. The income was designated for the purchase of recent art (Jackson 2007).

The imprecise character of museum governance documents relating to collections result in variable discussions when it comes to deciding what to acquire, what to keep, and what to remove. It is not unusual for museums to have things that are mission irrelevant only because they were acquired and accessioned once upon a time. The fact of ownership alone can be a deterrent to object departure, no matter how inexplicable its retention may be. People responsible for museums will be reluctant to dispose of collections out of fears that they were initially acquired for good reasons that escape current thinking.

Discussions surrounding the mission focus of collections must be exhaustively engaged in when considering deaccessioning. One exercise worth doing is to write a short "pretend narrative" exhibition label for an object. Will the label make it immediately obvious to the average gallery visitor why the item is in the particular museum? Recognizing that art museum labels are succinct and science museum labels veer in the opposite direction, the exercise is nevertheless worth pursuing. Perhaps the idea should be expanded to draft paragraphs that might appear in written materials explaining the *direct* value of something for a particular museum. If the outcome of these exercises simply suggests an item is "illustrative of" or "the sort of thing that might . . ." or "in keeping with . . . ," it may be too tangential to retain in a museum's collection.

Occasionally, an object completely irrelevant to a museum's mission

Figure 3.1.   *Artemis and the Stag.* Roman, first century BC–first century AD, bronze, deaccessioned by the Albright-Knox Gallery, Buffalo, New York, in 2007, now in a private collection. Photo by Steven Miller.

might remain in its collection simply because it has obvious commercial value and/or independent status of obvious import. A painting by Cezanne might be owned and shown at an automobile museum. A collection of Faberge eggs might be in a whaling museum. A Tiffany lamp collection might be found in a stamp museum. In addition, things are kept for political reasons. An item might have been donated by a prominent local figure, and no one has the nerve to suggest it be deaccessioned. Anyone with even the slightest sense of museum acquisition logic and discipline will, on the surface at least, find these dichotomies completely irregular. But collection anomalies are sometimes accepted in institutional cultures. They can be hard to correct regardless of obviously logical arguments to the contrary.

Retention Cost

Museum collections are expensive to own. Storage, conservation, research, and exhibitions cost money. Those unfamiliar with how museums operate will be ignorant of the real financial impact objects have on budgets. Facilities allocated to collection storage need to be built and maintained. Climate controls must be in place. Exhibits are hardly cheap. Staff qualified to work with collections are necessary. Because exhibitions are rarely static, changes occur, and those have price tags.

Operating budgets have an impact on collection retention and removal. Increasingly questions are being asked about the value, wisdom, and necessity of keeping all the things museums own. Good stewardship requires trained collection management and curatorial staff, safe storage and handling areas, and a commitment to conservation and long-term care. Museums, especially those located in cities, rarely have enough space to meet their needs.

The cost of keeping collections can become an issue when museums are in dire financial straits; people see income potential in what a museum owns. Cumulatively, collection retention costs are substantial. Questions may be asked about how the stuff can "pay" for its survival. Every so often those in authority think there must be some sort of measurable "monetary return on the investment" museums devote to collections. Unsatisfactory answers can result in the departure of "deadbeat" collections. This might especially be the case with large objects such as boats, cars, horse-drawn vehicles, and locomotives. It can be difficult to justify the cost of having and preserving these, in spite of mission relevancy.

Collection magnitude is a serious issue for many museums. It will only increase as storage facilities continue to fill, new buildings and additions become obsolete, and acquisition approaches fail to slow collection expansion.

Ceasing to collect runs counter to museum purposes and curatorial inclinations. Temporarily suspending acquisition activities simply postpones collection growth. Balancing incoming with outgoing collections is a peculiar notion that in practice rarely works. The thought that nothing should be added to a museum's collection unless something is subtracted from it is impractical to say the least. Regardless, collection increase will be a lurking if not growing argument for deaccessioning.

Storage Challenge

Though collection storage may be the least appreciated of a museum's duties, it is one of the most important responsibilities. To acquire things and fail to house them properly is totally irresponsible. How they are housed is critical to their care. Great museums, of any size, have great collections, and their institutional reputations reflect this. It is not unusual for these stellar collections to be many in number and often in storage.

A museum is a "library" of three-dimensional documents. Extensive and relevant museum collections are invaluable for research, study, scholarship, and, yes, exhibition. The library analogy is apt and should be applied when people question the meaning of storage. No one walks into a library and bemoans the fact that the vast majority of books it owns are not being read. Again, so it is with great libraries as with great museums. Typically, the larger and better the collection, the loftier the organization's reputation.

When certain museums do engage in deaccessioning, the reason put forth is that the things to be removed cost too much to store. The argument may or may not have merit. Criticisms about how much museums spend to properly retain permanent collections tend to come from people who do not understand the aesthetic, documentary, emotional, informational, or spiritual role of objects in a museum context, especially those held in any magnitude. Perplexed annoyance can be expressed about storage. The assumption is that because they are off exhibition they are not earning their keep. Countering the antistorage argument is tough. Allies are necessary, and these are usually understanding colleagues, sympathetic trustees, and guidelines issued by museum profession organizations such as the American Alliance of Museums or the American Association for State and Local History. Explaining the possibility of a public relations backlash if dormant collections are deaccessioned does no harm either. Confusion about collection storage must be confronted. Regular reminders of its importance and a protective stance against assaults are necessary.

Science museums offer excellent examples of museums with huge collections rarely seen by the public. These specimens have value for research and indeed have been carefully acquired over the years for this exact purpose. They offer a font of actual and potential information about our natural environment. The fact that they are in storage is immaterial when it comes to their scholarly importance.

Museums that fail to provide adequate, if perhaps not exemplary, collection storage fall short of fundamental responsibilities. Such circumstances inevitably implicate boards of trustees who have clearly failed to protect the treasures for which they are stewards. Trustees often dodge being held accountable for egregious institutional faults. They especially try to avoid spending much of their own money correcting problems. If the choice is to personally contribute to improved collection storage or reduce the volume of items stored, the latter will prevail if there are no other funding alternatives.

Ignorance of an Item

Occasionally museum collections are deaccessioned because a museum has no information about them. Contributing to this action are assumptions that information cannot be gotten, or such work is hardly worth the effort, or it is far too costly.

Research, scholarship, access, and good record keeping are essential aspects of responsible collection care. This has a cost. With the alarming increase in exhibition schedules and the need to fill galleries with changing installations, studying collections simply for the sake of learning is difficult for employees to do. In fact, some of this work is now almost pursued covertly by staff.

There is much to be learned from the things museums own. The educational potential of collections is enormous. Media alerts about discoveries revealed by research into collections are frequent. As noted, studies of natural history collections can be especially important as they expose previously unknown information about aspects of the world and even the universe it occupies. A painting thought to be by an unknown artist might in time be ascribed to a famous artist. Dormant history collections can suddenly become relevant as new aspects of the past and changing demographics and audience interests demand more expanded and inclusive museum research. We have certainly seen this in the area of African-American studies.

There is an expense to studying collections. Such academic exercises tend to have no immediately applicable practical outcomes. This reality can halt research while other institutional priorities dominate. As collections languish, untended intellectually, arguments can be made that since they are not earning their keep informationally, they should be deaccessioned. Sometimes it is easier to get rid of collections than to seek and retain knowledge about them.

Conservation Is Untenable

Conserving museum collections can be formidably expensive. There are two aspects to this duty: direct-care contact on collections and establishing a neutral and safe environment for collections. Applied physical actions are usually performed by qualified conservators. Safe environments include such things as cabinets, boxes, envelopes, shelving, secure climate-controlled rooms, and buildings that cannot pose threats to collections. In addition to conservators, designated staff can be trained in how to properly handle objects. (It is essential to note that this handling will not qualify them to be conservators.) Considering the poor survival options things face in the real world, even the simple fact of being in a museum helps assure a certain longevity for objects. However, the cost of holding collections responsibly is hardly insignificant.

Most museum collections are kept in a reasonable manner. This circumstance will improve as professional museum disciplines continue to improve. Considerable strides have already been made. Poor storage in many museums has been eliminated, or at least the necessity for doing so is recognized and the future is promising. Employees trained to handle collections are increasingly sought, and their authority is growing. Governing bodies (e.g., boards of trustees) know they have a duty to be mindful of the cultural riches entrusted to them.

As with so many other aspects of museums, conservation as a professional discipline and specialized duty has matured dramatically in the past several decades. What was once a craft at best or a janitorial function at worst is now a highly refined science and practice. This is a welcome development. It is also costly. Given the realization that museum collections often require substantial conservation attention, museums may decide these measures cannot be paid for and deaccessioning must be done.

Ownership Dispute

The vast majority of museum collections are possessed legally. When, on occasion, this may not be the case, deaccessioning can happen. An object will be transferred to its (presumably) rightful owner. Changes in possession can happen for several reasons. Individuals or groups can assure valid ownership. New laws are written that cause collection departures. In the United States, the most notable of these is the Native American Graves Protection and Repatriation Act, which requires museums receiving federal support to offer to return to federally recognized American Indian tribes human remains and objects of spiritual and cultural significance. Other laws support claims of restitution by individuals and heirs for art stolen by the Nazis in the 1930s and 1940s. The Holocaust Expropriated Art Recovery Act (HEAR) received unanimous support in Congress in December 2016. And there is a growing legal arena to reclaim cultural patrimony that countries declare was illicitly taken from them either recently or in the distant past, even if the taking happened before they became the nations they are now. Many African countries which at some point were European colonies fit this category.

Changes in moral conventions and ethical practices within the museum field itself can cause collection ownership reversals. This would be true for human remains once obtained as tourist souvenirs, curious decorations, or for spurious scientific study and at some point later acquired by a museum. That sort of collecting is now largely rejected as irresponsible and disrespectful.

An external claim of ownership for a museum collection item requires proof on the part of the claimant. Older museums might have few or no records documenting the acquisition of things in their collections. This may make it hard to substantiate institutional ownership. Yet museums should never deaccession an object without confirmation of the justification of a demand. Possession alone is often a legitimate argument for retention.

Substantiated evidence of ownership should be expected by both the museum and the supplicant. Disputes can be quite vitriolic. They can unfold over a long time. They can also be settled quickly and amicably. Qualified legal advice is important to seek when the circumstances of an ownership question are debatable.

Collection Duplication

Sometimes having museum collections that are exactly alike can result in deaccessioning. This is especially true for prints and photographs. These artistic mediums are specifically designed to allow original copies to be produced in multiples, be they from engraved metal plates, lithography stones, silkscreens, or negatives. There might be several or a slew of original photographs made by a photographer from the same negative. Similarly, caution is advised because what might appear to be a duplicate print could simply be another "state" of a particular print. Regardless of when these were done, or even by whom, some can see these (literally) as duplicates.

Collection duplication occurs with other things museums collect. A historical society could inexplicably own a bunch of nineteenth-century Thonet bentwood café chairs, all made the same way at the same time and looking alike. There may be several pairs of an identical shoe model in a museum's costume collection. A military museum might have more than a handful of 45-caliber World War II Remington pistols. Many specimen samples of a plant can be in a science museum.

The concept of the unique or the multiple and how that may affect deaccessioning is critical to understand. There are inherent multiplicity possibilities that need to be assessed carefully when considering removal. A historic church with lots of matching pews would hardly think of getting rid of the majority because they are duplicates. However, a huge pile of such matching pews removed from a long-gone church and acquired and accessioned by a museum, though having no useful mission application or reason to be preserved and taking up valuable storage space, might be perfect candidates for deaccessioning.

A few years ago, a large urban history museum deaccessioned numerous photographs taken by a famous American photographer. They were fourth, fifth, or even sixth copies produced at the time when the original negatives were made. The photos were sold at a well-known auction house. The source of each was clearly noted in the catalogue, as was the fact that funds realized by the sale would accrue to the benefit of the museum's collections. The museum retained at least two photographs from each negative, which it held and still does. Because there were so many "duplicates" and they all "looked alike," the decision to sell the "surplus" was easy for the director and board to make.

Assessments of duplicates can be substantial or superficial. To avoid mistakes, care is advised. A set of dishes or silverware will contain many duplicates, but it would be silly for a historic house museum to dispose of them. Having lots of robins' eggs may at first seem duplicitous in a science museum, but they could hold unique research value.

Redundancy

There is a collection retention argument that differentiates between what is duplicate and what is redundant. *Redundancy* as a deaccession category is more likely to include things similar or closely related in scope, content, appearance, relevance, materials, application, origin, or subject. Having an overabundance of a particular sort of collection can lead to discussions about the necessity or wisdom of keeping most of it. Museums might feel they are "top heavy" in certain holdings. Some institutions want more balance in their collections or feel a need to fill gaps. An automobile museum may decide it has too many cars from the 1950s and not enough from the 1960s. A regional preservation organization responsible for all sorts of historic buildings could decide it has too many. A natural history museum might want to reduce its collection of shells and seek more snake skins.

Citing redundancy as a reason for deaccessioning can be obvious or not. The automobile museum officials might think it has too many cars from the 1950s, but visitors may disagree. A perceived redundancy could simply suggest a new acquisition emphasis. Rather than get rid of cars from the 1950s, get more from the 1960s. On the other hand, it might be entirely clear to everyone that the historic preservation organization has too many buildings and some should be deaccessioned. ("Accessioning" buildings in the same manner as smaller museum collections is a larger subject, outside the immediate and practical purview of this discussion. Suffice to say, buildings can indeed have accession numbers and thus qualify to be deaccessioned as herein described.) As for a natural history museum having too many shells and not enough snake skins, the public is probably unaware of a particular collection magnitude or application and probably not care. They will be aware of large items like dinosaur fossils and skeletons on exhibit. Quite a ruckus will erupt if these are deaccessioned with unfounded alacrity simply because museum officials see something as redundant.

There is no hard and fast rule for defining redundancy in a museum. It is a subjective contextual exercise based on an individual institution's collection philosophy, objectives, and operating realities as articulated by those in positions of knowledge, authority, and responsibility (not always a common combination of traits, by the way).

Fake or Forgery

Public narratives offered in and by museums largely happen through collections as presented in exhibitions. Objects are assigned the duty of embodying information about subjects. Those subjects can focus on people, places, events, ideas, epochs, concepts—you name it. Museum collections provide evidence that acts as proof. Collections substantiate missions. Objects are three-dimensional documents confirming or proving the veracity of points of view, meanings, opinions, and perspectives.

The "fact messenger" task of museum collections is apparent in exhibitions, research documents, publications, accession records, and more. The confirmation of collection value is based on their credibility as objects about a subject under discussion. Forgeries, fakes, and spurious objects can be disruptive to the authenticity of a museum narrative. It is why great care is taken during an acquisition process to confirm the "honesty" of whatever is being considered for the permanent collection. It is also a reason for deaccessioning something found to lack physical or content honesty.

For the most part, most museum collections are what they are said to be. Once in a while that turns out not to be the case. When something is discovered to be a fake, forgery, or of specious inherent physical or content integrity, deaccessioning might be suggested, though not always. A famous fake by a famous faker could remain in a museum for informational purposes relating to its mission. An example of this might be an art museum keeping a painting by the notorious Dutch artist Han van Meegeren (1889–1947), who made paintings he fobbed off on Nazi leaders as being by Vermeer. They fell for the frauds (Lopez 2008).

Recognizing if a collection item is a fake or forgery can be easy or require the expertise of a specialist. Great care is necessary when reviewing collections for bogus content. If something is a known fake and a museum fails to acknowledge that fact, its reputation for academic integrity suffers. On the other hand, there have been examples of museum objects once thought authentic that were exposed as fakes only to be later reauthenticated.

In science museums, questions of authenticity can hover around the identity of specimens represented in collections. What once might have been considered a Mastodon bone might, with additional information and upon further research, prove to be something else. The museum's interest in retaining the bone may dissolve.

In 2017 the Mexican Museum of San Francisco announced that only eighty-three of the two thousand artifacts in its pre-Hispanic or pre-Columbian era collection could be authenticated, a news story by the Associated Press that was widely reported in numerous publications. The museum planned to remove the 1,917 suspects by donating them to schools and for other educational purposes (Associated Press 2017a, 2017b).

Museums purport to be about truth. They have assigned themselves the job of presenting what they consider real stories about subjects they think have value and importance. Being human endeavors, museum perspectives are subjective. Regardless, every object on view is used to attest to a particular exhibition subject. The tangible connects us to the intangible. The real thing is a messenger of veracity. If an art work, historic artifact, or scientific specimen is a fake, its job to convince is compromised.

Copies or Reproductions

Somewhat related to questions about fakes or forgeries in a museum collection are concerns about accessioned copies or reproductions. The discussions should center on the original intent of the copy or reproduction and why it was accessioned to begin with. A museum might have every reason to want and keep a drawing by an important twenty-first-century artist that is a copy of a Michelangelo drawing. A historic house containing twentieth-century copies of Chippendale-style dining chairs that are original to the house and its modern occupants may be retained. On the other hand, copies or reproductions that are simply in a museum as exhibition props and were accessioned for no valid reason may be of little long-term ownership value and might be candidates for deaccessioning.

Accessioning known copies and reproductions is an acceptable museum practice when some aspect of the item is mission appropriate. Presumably the reproduction or copy fact is noted in the records along with why it was acquired and numbered. When such items are accepted by a museum for noncollection reasons, there is usually no need to assign them customary museum accession numbers. Copies and reproductions are often used in hands-on educational fashion. When an inventory system is in place for this allocation, it must be different from permanent collection accession systems.

Deaccessioning a copy or reproduction changes an object's museum retention purpose. It may leave a museum entirely. It might be kept for some practical purpose. This could include use as office décor, a hands-on teaching prop, or for sale in the gift shop.

Poor Quality

Issues of quality involving collections include their physical condition and informational value. When either or both are questionable, subpar, or lacking entirely, deaccessioning might be an option. The poor condition of an object is usually readily apparent. It is falling apart, and there may be no valid reason to pursue a museum's preservation imperative to conserve, restore, or otherwise save it. Of course, some things in bad repair need to be kept regardless of condition. The woefully deteriorated American flag that inspired Francis Scott Key to write the nation's national anthem and is on exhibit at the Smithsonian Institution in Washington, DC, immediately comes to mind.

Assessing the physical quality or informational value of a museum object is best done by staff or consultants with knowledge relevant to the object and its documentary content. Deaccession decisions resulting from such assessments are at the option of the owning museum. As always, documenting the process and outcomes is important.

Exhibition Absence

An argument used for deaccessioning rests on the fact that an object has not been exhibited for a long time, or ever. This is compounded by assumptions that there will be no exhibition opportunities in the foreseeable future, or ever. The removal suggestion rests on the idea that collections exist only to be seen by the public in the form of an exhibition.

The exhibition function of objects in museums is secondary to their content purpose. A museum's preservation imperative rarely if ever always references exhibition as a constant and singular collecting and retention raison d'être. Moreover, failures to exhibit something are usually not determined by the cultural value or material importance of an object. Exhibition absence most likely results from limited funding for staff, space, and programs as well as condition issues, employee interest, and trustee preferences.

Exhibits are expensive. Staff, space, and schedules preclude placing a majority of most museum collections on view all the time or even in some temporary rotating fashion. More to the point, and emphasizing the preservation role museums play, some items should not be exposed to the light of day or any other kind of light for long, if at all. These materials include art and documents on paper, textiles and fabrics, or certain animal specimens. There is a reason that Cezanne watercolors are rarely exhibited. A dark space is necessary for showing the aforementioned American flag at the Smithsonian Institution. Beautiful butterflies will lose their iridescent wing coloring if exposed to light for too long.

In addition to conservation issues, the very size of a particular collection can reduce exhibition frequency. This is especially true with large collections of prints and photographs. The sheer volume makes them difficult to exhibit in their entirety or even often. The Museum of the City of New York holds one of the most important collections of lithographs by the New York City nineteenth-century sequential publishing firms of N. Currier and Currier & Ives. Of the three thousand prints, few have been seen on exhibition by visitors over the years. (However, they have been widely reproduced in scores of publications over the years.) The same is true for the Library of Congress, which has a similar size collection of pictures by the same companies. Deciding to keep either of these holdings based on their limited exhibition histories has, fortunately, not been contemplated by either repository.

Science museums are awash in collections rarely seen in an exhibition context. Dead insects, birds, and other preserved animals are held for research purposes. The same is true for gems, minerals, and rocks of all sorts that fill storage facilities. Butterfly and bird egg collections are extensive. All have actual or potentially rich informational value. This is especially true as climates change radically, and these collections might be DNA time capsules of past or vanishing environmental conditions. Given the scholarly basis for natural history collections, exhibits are often a secondary reason to have them.

An example of deaccession threats to science museum collections happened when the Academy of Natural Science in Philadelphia considered selling its gem and mineral collection in 2006 to fix a terrible financial mess. The move was so controversial it helped lead to the merger of the Academy with Drexel University in 2011. Now known as the Academy of Natural Sciences of Drexel University, its operational health is much improved. More to the point, its vast collections remain in a public repository (Academy of Natural Sciences and Drexel University 2011).

Archaeology collections are rarely exhibited either in part or in their entirety. This is especially true for excavated materials acquired in the field in mass quantities. Museums holding these materials are responsible for yards and yards of shelved boxes containing all manner of things dug out of the earth, including some of that earth. As with the aforementioned geology collection, deaccessioning archaeologically recovered items can be done, but it is fraught with potential peril if professional protocols are violated.

Source of Income

It is not unusual for museums to see collections as a source of income. In these instances, selling museum collections is done for obvious reasons—to make money. The income can be put to various uses, including the purchase of new acquisitions, the direct conservation of objects, general operating costs, underwriting capital expenses, or paying debt. Most museum profession organizations and most museums recommend or require the income from collection sales be assigned to collecting and/ or conservation. This is done for two reasons. It reinforces the concept of the museum as first and foremost a collection-based endeavor, the contents of which are sustained for past, present, and future generations. And it reduces the practice of selling things to pay operating, capital, or loan costs.

As remarked upon elsewhere, decisions to sell things and how to use the proceeds rest with boards of trustees. However, as with all deaccessioning, it is imperative that museum records and pertinent laws be reviewed for restrictions regarding possible deaccession actions and outcomes. Few laws, government regulations, or statutes mandate when, how, and with what results commercial deaccessioning can happen. New York State has deaccessioning legislation that must be adhered to by museums chartered by the state (Cash 2011; Patterson Belknap Webb & Tyler LLP 2012); the New York State Museum developed "A Sample Collections Management Policy" for New York museums to follow state law (appendix II). Endangered species legislation restricts sales of certain materials such as ivory. Care is demanded when deaccessioning "live" munitions, salacious materials, items that might contribute to illicit markets, things containing toxic substances, or objects deemed controversial.

Safety Threat

Few people think museum collections pose physical threats, be it to themselves, other collections, facilities, or people. Yet on occasion accessioned objects may be dangerous. "Live" munitions might be included in history museums' collections. Old taxidermy mounts stuffed with arsenic, mercury, or lead can be found in natural history collections. Some film-based early-twentieth-century photograph negatives can self-immolate. History and science museums may have containers holding mysterious and highly toxic chemicals. Such content can be in contemporary artworks. The option to deaccession these and similar collections is always a possibility. Sometimes they deaccession themselves. In the interest of safeguarding future owners, museums are cautioned to understand and explain the potential or actual volatile nature of what they are removing. Advice may be sought from local authorities trained to oversee the disposal of hazardous materials. This may be the case when asbestos is found during renovation projects in old museum structures. Museums must never deaccession hazardous collections in an unsafe manner.

Appropriate for Another Museum

Intermuseum ownership transfer of collections is not unusual. This happens when a museum feels art, artifacts, or specimens are more relevant to another institution. This also happens when a museum cannot or does not want to keep an item but wants it to stay in the public sector. Occasionally, even though an object may be mission relevant to a museum, the public might be better served were it in another museum.

The aforementioned Egyptian antiquities collected by the nineteenth-century British physician Dr. Henry Abbott that made its way from his museum to the New-York Historical Society to the Brooklyn Museum offers a good illustration of intermuseum collection transfer (Maurita 2011). In 2014, Boscobel Restoration, Inc., in Garrison, New York, deaccessioned by gift to the United States Military Academy at West Point a mid-nineteenth-century painting of that site (see figure 3.2) (see appendix III, Media Alert: Boscobel House and Gardens). On a much larger scale, in 2009 the Metropolitan Museum of Art accessioned the costume collection of the Brooklyn Museum (Glier 2010). Another commendable ownership change happened when the Museum of the City of New York gave two historic period rooms to two other

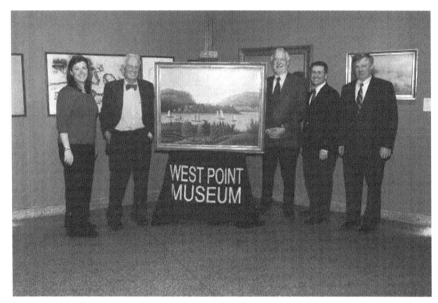

Figure 3.2. Officials posing with a mid-1850s painting of West Point, deaccessi-oned by Boscobel Restoration, Inc., in Garrison, New York, USA, in 2014 and given to the West Point Museum at the United States Military Academy. Photo courtesy Steven Miller.

museums (see chapter 6 for more information) (Antiques and the Arts Weekly 2009).

Unable to Meet Acquisition Restrictions

Museums prefer to own collections unfettered by donor restrictions. These binding agreements dictate aspects of what can or cannot be done with a gift. Avoiding restrictions is customary acquisition practice now. There were exceptions in the past as donors would require, and museums would accept, ownership encumbrances. (To be sure, this happens still, though with far less frequency.) Museums usually abide by such arrange-ments. When they fail to do so, prefer not to, or cannot, deaccessioning might result. Often the action is preceded by legal processes. Objects might be returned to owners or heirs or transferred to another institution that can abide by original gift restrictions. Occasionally restrictions can be totally or partially rescinded through legal mechanisms. In these rare instances, deaccessioning may be avoided altogether.

Stolen, Destroyed, or Missing Item

Collection security is a primary responsibility for museums. Unfortunately, accessioned art, historic artifacts, or scientific specimens can be lost through theft, natural disaster (e.g., fire, flood, earthquake), manmade destruction, or discovered missing for inexplicable reasons. An example of manmade destruction occurred when ISIS destroyed the second largest museum in Iraq in 2015; the abominable act was filmed by ISIS and covered widely in the news, including the video being aired on TV (Associated Press 2015; Mohammed 2015).

These losses can be considered a form of deaccessioning. The designation is applied at the option of an individual museum. Ironically, museums themselves can participate in "deaccessioning by destruction." A good example happens as certain scientific specimens are demolished when sampling for research purposes. Museum records must reflect these losses and include official acknowledgment by the board of trustees.

Violation of Conflict-of-Interest Policy

It happens rarely, but on occasion deaccessioning may occur because it was discovered that an acquisition violated a museum's conflict-of-interest policy, or one it must abide by if it is part of a larger entity (as might be the case with museums owned by governments, universities, or commercial businesses). To be sure, the policy should usually have been in effect when the questionable acquisition took place. The reasons for such violations can vary. Staff may have known at the time of the acquisition that it was a conflict of interest and that barrier was ignored on purpose or circumvented for whatever reason. The conflict may have been unknown at the time of the acquisition and discovered or revealed afterward.

Whether purposeful or innocent, the motivation for violating a conflict-of-interest policy will need to be recorded to the best of a museum's ability as it implements this kind of deaccession. Of course, any potential legal entanglements or consequences need to be investigated. If these exist the deaccessioning process will take them into consideration. If there are none, it can proceed as outlined elsewhere in this book.

In 2017, a museum in the southeastern United States was alerted to a possible conflict-of-interest acquisition practice. On a regular basis a staff member of the museum unilaterally exhibited and acquired for the permanent collection art by that person's lover. The museum imprimatur provided a high-profile commercial advantage for the artist. It was featured in the person's regular public relations alerts including advertising, targeted mailings, a website, blogs, events, and social media. To increase the value of an art and an artist, "The surest way by far is [with] an exhibition in the right museums and, even better, incorporation into their collection" (Bunzl 2014, 66). No other artists in that city enjoyed such a cozy association with the museum. In fact, it was difficult if not impossible for them to have their work shown or acquired, even by gift. When frustrated employees confidentially brought the highly irregular intimate arrangement to the attention of officials, those in authority immediately recognized it as a blatant personal as well as professional conflict of interest. At the time of this writing a considered solution was to deaccession the art in question, return it to the artist, and cease acquiring and exhibiting any more from that source (confidential email to author).

Unpopular Item

On occasion, an item or items will be deaccessioned by a museum because it or they are disliked by an influential trustee or employee. The action is often rationalized (camouflaged?) with reasons gerrymandered from the list outlined above.

Combination of Reasons

It is not unusual for museums to remove items for a combination of the above mentioned reasons. This was the case when the Metropolitan Museum of Art deaccessioned items at a Christie's auction in 2015. The introduction to the catalogue, written by a museum staff member, noted:

> So this has been just the right moment thoroughly to reassess our British collections for the first time in half a century. We have done so thinking about what stories arise from which objects, and more practically how much space we will have in our galleries, and indeed our storerooms. Judge Untermyer [the donor of the majority of items deaccessioned] was keen to see his pieces displayed, if not continuously, then at least

sometimes. Even at the inaugural exhibition of his collection, however, the Met was able to show only about 400 of the works he had given or bequeathed. Moreover, as the Met's collections have grown, some duplication has been inevitable. In areas of particular richness, we plan to rotate the installations. But, though we expect to move objects on and off display more frequently than at present, without our review and this sale, there would still be pieces that sadly would never see the light of day. And if we have more than we need in certain areas, there is not enough material in others. So this has also been the opportunity to identify gaps in our collection—for example in the nineteenth century, from Regency to the Great Exhibition to Arts and Crafts Movement and Design Reform. With the proceeds of this sale we hope to fill those gaps, acquiring objects that will be shown alongside masterpieces from the Cadwalader, Sage, Pell, Lockwood, Cohn and, above all, Untermeyer collections. (Syson 2015, 11)

The deaccession reasons cited above include removing duplicate art, selling things because they had not been on view, and storage and exhibition space was problematic. The catalogue notice also explained that the proceeds were to be used for acquisitions.

There are many reasons for museums to deaccession collections. Some are accepted and make sense. Others may be questioned. Those agreeing with deaccession decisions can be found inside and outside a museum. It is therefore incumbent on an institution to set clear guidelines for how it removes items from its possession. And it is essential that museum leaders approve such action formally and officially for the record well advance of the departure of an object.

References

Academy of Natural Sciences and Drexel University. 2011. "The Academy of Natural Sciences and Drexel Announce Historic Affiliation." DrexelNOW, May 19, 2011. drexel.edu/now/archive/2011/May/The-Academy-of-Natural-Sciences-Announce-an-Historic-Affiliation/.

Antiques and the Arts Weekly. 2009. "Museum of City of New York Donates Rockefeller Rooms." *Antiques and the Arts Weekly*, April 7, 2009. http://www.antiquesandthearts.com/museum-of-city-of-new-york-donates-rockefeller-rooms/.

Associated Press. 2015. "ISIS Video Shows Militants Smashing Ancient Iraq Artifacts." CBSNews.com, February 26. https://www.cbsnews.com/news/isis-video-shows-militants-smashing-ancient-iraq-artifacts/.

———. 2017a. "Majority of Museum Collection Fails Authentication." *US News*, July 7. https://www.usnews.com/news/best-states/california/articles/2017-07-07/majority-of-museum-collection-fails-authentication.

———. 2017b. "Majority of Museum Collection Fails Authentication." *Washington Times*, July 7. http://www.washingtontimes.com/news/2017/jul/7/majority-of-museum-collection-fails-authentication/.

Bunzl, Matti. 2014. *In Search of a Lost Avant-Garde: An Anthropologist Investigates the Contemporary Art Museum.* Chicago: University of Chicago Press, 2014.

Cash, Stephanie. 2011. "New York Clarifies Museum Deaccessions." *Art in America*, May 18. http://www.artinamericamagazine.com/news-features/news/amendment-deaccession/.

Glier, Jan. 2010. *High Style: Masterworks from the Brooklyn Museum Costume Collection at the Metropolitan Museum of Art* (Exhibit Catalogue). New York: Reeder and Metropolitan Museum of Art.

Jackson, Bruce. 2007. "The War Against the Albright-Knox." *Artvoice* 6, no. 8 (February 22). http://artvoice.com/issues/v6n8/war_against_the_albright_knox.html.

Lopez, Jonathan. 2008. *The Man Who Made Vermeers: Unvarnishing the Legend of Master Forger Han van Meegeren.* Orlando, FL: Harcourt.

Maurita. 2011. "Egypt on Broadway." *From the Stacks. New-York Historical Society Museum Library* (blog). September 19, 2011. http://blog.nyhistory.org/egypt-on-broadway/.

Mohammed, Riyadh. 2015. "ISIS Destroys Second Largest Museum in Iraq." *The Fiscal Times*, February 26. http://www.thefiscaltimes.com/2015/02/26/ISIS-Destroys-Second-Largest-Museum-Iraq.

Patterson Belknap Webb & Tyler LLP. 2012. "New York Board of Regents Adopts New Deaccessioning Rules." *Lexology*, August 28. https://www.lexology.com/library/detail.aspx?g=569f91f1-5f52-4f6e-9025-539f1809f2d8.

Syson, Luke. 2015. "The British Collections at the Metropolitan Museum of Art." *American Collecting in the English Tradition, Property of the Metropolitan Museum of Art* (Auction Catalogue). October 27, 2015. New York: Christie's, 6–11.

Vogel, Carol. 2008. "Philadelphia Raises Enough Money to Retain a Masterpiece by Eakins." *New York Times*, April 24, 2008. www.nytimes.com/2008/04/24/arts/design/24gros.html.

DEACCESSION PROCESSES

I n the course of their daily operations, museums follow various processes. Among others, these include a process for opening and closing,
how to handle money at the admission desk and in offices, processes
for working with a range of employees, and collection management processes. A foremost collection management process will address the removal
of items from permanent ownership. This process, of course, is called
deaccessioning. It must be enumerated in no uncertain terms in an official
manner. It is usually defined as a policy and established and approved in
writing in governance documents.

Deaccession Policies

All museums need to have a deaccession policy. It should articulate formal, step-by-step procedures in writing. It is important that the policy be
board approved and codified in overall collection management practices,
though it may also be referenced in by-laws, annual audits, articles of
incorporation, or other official records. The specifics of these processes
will be in these governance documents (for an example, see appendix IV,
Metropolitan Museum of Art Deaccessioning Policy). Additional examples can be found online, some of which are mentioned in table 4.1.

As a "living document," the deaccession policy will require regular
review for potential updating. Adjustments would reflect alterations in a
museum's mission, changes in pertinent laws, new recommendations
within the museum profession, evolving ethical considerations about certain collections (as might be the case with human remains, for instance),
and any changes in collection retention priorities.

Optimally, a policy will explain that suggestions regarding deaccessioning should be generated by staff knowledgeable about relevant collections. These recommendations need to be made within the context of an

Table 4.1   Examples of Deaccession Policies

Institution	URL
Art Gallery of Ontario. AGO Deaccessioning Policy	http://www.ago.net/ago-deaccessioning -policy
Cincinnati Museum Center Collections Policy. VII. Deaccession and Disposition	https://www.cincymuseum.org/sites/default/ files/Collections%20Policy,%20March%2010, %202011.pdf
Dallas Museum of Art. Criteria for the Deaccession of Artworks	https://www.dma.org/art-deaccessioned -artworks/criteria-deaccession-artworks
Dartmouth University Hood Museum of Art. Deaccession	http://hoodmuseum.dartmouth.edu/explore/ collection/policies-image-requests/ deaccession
Museum of Applied Arts & Sciences. MAAS Deaccession Policy	https://maas.museum/app/uploads/2016/09/ MAAS-Deaccession-Policy.pdf
Museums & Galleries of NSW. Deaccessioning and Disposal	https://mgnsw.org.au/sector/resources/ online-resources/collection-management/ deaccessioning-and-disposal/
National Park Service. Museum Management Program. *NPS Museum Handbook, Part II: Museum Records.* Chapter 6. Deaccessioning.	https://www.nps.gov/museum/publications/ MHII/mh2ch6.pdf
Shiloh Museum of Ozark History. Deaccession Policy	http://download.aaslh.org/StEPs + Resources/ Deaccession + Policy + Shiloh + Museum.pdf
Smithsonian Anacostia Community Museum. Deaccession Plan and Workflow	http://anacostia.si.edu/resources/ ManagementDocuments/MicrosoftWord -Document22DeaccessionPolicy.pdf
University of Alaska, Museum of the North. UAMN Collections Management Policy, VII. Deaccessioning and Disposal	https://www.uaf.edu/museum/collections/ ethno/policies/deaccessioning/
University of Alberta. Deaccession and Disposition of Museum Objects and Collections Procedure	https://policiesonline.ualberta.ca/ PoliciesProcedures/Procedures/Deaccession -and-Disposition-of-Museum-Objects-and -Collections-Procedure.pdf
University of Alaska, Museum of the North. UAMN Collections Management Policy, VII. Deaccessioning and Disposal	https://www.uaf.edu/museum/collections/ ethno/policies/deaccessioning/
University of New Mexico, Museum of Southwestern Biology. Accession and Deaccession	http://msb.unm.edu/about-us/museum -policies/accession-and-deaccession/ index.html

institution's mission and how that is realized through what it owns. Lead staff tend to be curators, but they may also include registrars, conservators, and directors. The advice and guidance provided must be intellectually sound and operationally practical. If employees lack the requisite experience and skills for this task, outside opinions are sought. Even if staff are well versed in a museum's collections, external input can be an essential part of a deaccession process.

If a deaccession recommendation does not come from collection-oriented employees knowledgeable about what is being disposed of, their input and opinions must be seriously considered anyway. Occasionally, when this does not happen, unfortunate collection departures occur. If the board of trustees is requiring an unwise deaccession, staff or outside consultants may have little recourse but to concur regardless of professional position or opinion. This is also the case when laws or legal actions require a museum to give up ownership of an object. Such might happen when a stolen item is discovered to be in a collection and its original owner or legitimate heir successfully seeks its return. The role of professional staff is obviously negated when deaccessioning occurs by theft, unplanned destruction, trustee whim, or the closing of a museum.

Deaccessioning should never be done unilaterally, by one person, absent the involvement of other parties holding positions of responsibility for the museum undertaking the action. Even all-volunteer organizations or those with only one or two paid employees will usually have governance structures that officially engage and give authority to designated representatives—plural. For the most part, in addition to staff, these will be members of a board of trustees.

The three parts of a museum deaccession policy require deliberative processes for:

- recommending

- approving

- implementing

To be officially reviewed and acted upon, a deaccession proposal should be put in writing. An informal conversation or agreement is an unacceptable way to delete things. Documentation needs to describe what is being removed, why, and how. Avoid uninformative explanations such as "Lots of pieces of china stored in boxes in the attic." Include accession records or a link to them. Photographs that provide clear and obvious imagery of the objects in question are essential. Finally, the reason or reasons for suggesting the removal must be explained. This can be as simple as, "The object has self-destructed" or "The object is totally outside the mission, collecting scope, educational, or other use for the museum." Or, it can be more nuanced:

- "The museum has ten similar items and this one is the most overtly redundant and least important."

- "There is no research, exhibition, or preservation value to it and it is reasonable to assume none will accrue in the future."

- "The museum was forced to acquire it by an influential, long-deceased trustee (who left no heirs) who was seeking a tax donation at the end of the year it was given."

- "The museum cannot care for the object."

A deaccession proposal needs to outline the steps boards of trustees must follow in receiving, considering, and acting upon deaccession proposals. Recording the process as it unfolds is important and should be noted in meeting minutes and when decisions are made. A written proposal will usually include recommendations on how to proceed with the deaccession once it or part of it is approved.

Transparent deliberations are critical to nonprofit procedures, and especially for museums when they engage in removing collections. There are several ways to remove collections. The most common are by:

- sale

- gift

- exchange

- demotion

- destruction

- return

- transfer

- some combination of the above

These are discussed in detail in chapter 5.

Collection Committees

Museums of any size can and usually do have a trustee committee responsible for monitoring collections in various capacities. These may be known as the Collection Committee, Collection and Exhibition Committee, or Curatorial Committee. Whatever its name, duties tend to include: recommending for board approval all policies and practices relating to museum collections and/or exhibitions; suggesting, reviewing, and possibly approving exhibitions; responding to acquisition desires; monitoring collection conservation; setting research practices and standards for collections and exhibitions; and reviewing and approving deaccessions. If a museum is without this sort of governance oversight, it would be wise to establish the structure and list the committee's duties. The Museum Trustee Association (http://www.museumtrustee.org) can be of assistance in providing various templates. Contacting museums for samples of governance documents and collection management policies is also recommended. These may also be found on museum websites.

A written deaccession proposal is first presented to a designated board committee(s) (see appendix V). This can be done in confidence, but at some point, the outcome should be made known publicly. Seeing the actual items being submitted for deaccession is essential, though documentary photos can suffice for discussion purposes in certain situations and circumstances. Informed discussion must ensue about the plan of action.

According to staff at the National Gallery of Art, the gallery does not deaccession works of art other than selling duplicate prints; the Board of Trustees must approve such actions, and funds are only used to acquire other works of art (confidential email to author).

There are no stupid questions when it comes to exploring the ramifications of deleting collections. Even the simplest and most obvious of reasons might have unforeseen complications. Everyone deserves to be heard, but expert voices brought in at the beginning stages of a deaccession discussion should be given special credence. Board committees can have the authority to judge the qualifications of the personnel or appropriate volunteers or consultants asked to advise. Remember that while the vast majority of deaccessions are done without difficulty, it is essential to be mindful of potential controversy.

When staff and the pertinent board committees understand all aspects of a proposed deaccession and collection removal is recommended, the proposal should be given to the full board for final consideration and approval. Boards have several options when it comes to deaccessions. They can approve a proposal in its entirety, decline it, wait and ask for additional information, or if there is more than one object under consideration, divide the contents as deemed preferable and pursue a partial or sequential deaccession. Once a deaccession is approved by an institution's governing body, initiating, managing, and monitoring it must be done by designated qualified staff throughout the rest of the process.

Museum-Initiated Deaccession

As with accessioning, so with deaccessioning; it can be something of a subjective exercise. Adding or subtracting collections depends on decision makers arguing that an object is worth having or removing. Cogent arguments must be offered to justify either outcome. The more relevant and obvious they are, the better.

To reiterate, deaccession recommendations in museums should originate with museum personnel knowledgeable about the mission of the institution, its collections, and specific pieces within an area of the collection. Depending on the size and nature of the museum, there may be several staff members involved in initial recommendations. Occasionally consultants are brought in to offer opinions on objects. These people may be dealers, collectors, or staff from other museums. This was certainly the case in 2012 when a large urban history museum was vetting its jewelry collection and a major dealer in antique and designer jewelry was hired to assist curators with content and style identifications. The dealer did not make deaccession recommendations. He only provided information (personal observation by the author). Regardless of their role, consultants may offer ownership suggestions, but final retention or rejection decisions must be made by a museum's governing authority.

The curatorial role in deaccessioning should derive from the intellectual character of that job. Good museum curators will be familiar with most of the museum collections for which they are responsible. Assessing strengths and weaknesses in this arena is an ongoing part of the discipline. Most curators have a written and mental "wish list" of what they would like to add to a museum's collections, and they will understand what may be gotten rid of. Ideally their ruminations will be well codified and readily explained. Care is necessary before any decisions can or should be made, and lengthy discussions are advised that include additional relevant staff and trustees. Following this process, the reason for a deaccessioning will be easily understood and explained both internally at a museum and externally for the general public, media, or special interest groups.

It is not unusual for collection managers to suggest and/or be involved in recommending, reviewing, or commenting on deaccessioning. Often these "accountants for the collection" are more familiar with the overarching scope of an institution's diverse holdings than a curator of a particular segment, a director, or a trustee. Though collection managers may have no specific area of collection content expertise, if they have been with a museum a long time, they can be more than a little cognizant of all that has been acquired over the years. Moreover, they will probably be keenly aware of storage circumstances, collection use, records, and pertinent condition issues.

Conservators can help a museum make informed decisions about deaccessioning. These material experts usually know more about the stability, survival options, and physical integrity of designated collections than other museum staff or consultants. It is important to recognize that conservators specialize in various materials such as paper, paintings on canvas, metal, wood, ceramics, glass, and more. If condition is a deciding factor when reviewing museum collections for possible deaccessioning, unless an object is so obviously disintegrated or its condition otherwise clearly compromised even to the untrained eye, the advice of a conservator is wise to seek.

The role of the museum director in making deaccessioning decisions is critical to authorizing a final outcome. Some are well acquainted with a particular museum's collections. Others not so much. In either case, they should confidentially engage those with a relevant knowledge of a collection arena. Directors play the same operational role in the approval or denial process of deaccessioning as they do when a museum acquires something. It is unusual for directors to have the sole final authority in these deliberations. This will, or should, rest with the board of trustees. In their capacity as chief executives, directors need to confirm or deny the status of collections in possible flux. They should do this in writing even if that writing only involves a signature on relevant documents.

Final approval of deaccessioning should rest with a museum's board of trustees. For the most part these volunteers will have no or little knowledge of or about particular objects being removed from institutional ownership. Their decisions should thus be informed by in-depth documentation provided by staff, and possibly consultants, relevant specialists, or collectors who can authoritatively contribute to a removal conversation. Legal advice may also be sought. Once a decision is made, the results must be voted on by the full board and recorded in minutes and other pertinent governance documents. However a decision is made, such action is usually based on the reasons cited in chapter 3. Consequently, as staff, trustees, consultants, or other outside advisors examine, propose, and approve collection removals, the logic of their actions will be codified accordingly.

It is rare and usually wrong for a museum employee, trustee, or volunteer to independently deaccession something from a museum's collection. Most individuals have neither the authority nor knowledge to engage in the action. They may be unaware of, or wish to avoid, recommended processes, conventional documentation, and any legal parameters that must to be followed. They risk unknowingly eviscerating the contents of a museum, damaging its reputation, and putting themselves in a compromising position for implementing what could be thought, or is, an egregious conflict of interest. Their actions could even be illegal. Individuals should have no standing to remove collections unilaterally. If, on the other hand, a member of a museum's staff or board is aware of generally accepted museum profession deaccession procedures and chooses to "divest" an object from the "collection portfolio," perhaps something more nefarious and less innocent is happening.

Externally Initiated Museum Deaccession

Deaccessions thrust upon a museum by outside forces are those over which an institution has no control. Several examples of externally forced deaccessions can be cited. The Native American Graves Protection and Repatriation Art (NAGPRA) may call for ownership transfers of sacred and culturally significant artifacts claimed by officially recognized American Indian tribes. Repatriating art stolen by the Nazis during World War II, or acquired by forced sale, can be the outcome of legal actions and settlements. Collection destruction by outside human or natural forces comprise externally initiated collection loss. The dissolution, merger, or relocation of a museum can see the loss of collections or parts thereof. To be sure, under certain circumstances museums may challenge outside demands on collections. Occasionally museums succeed, but more often their defense is futile.

Monitoring, adhering to, or keeping records of deaccessions forced on museums will obviously vary according to the circumstances of each event. Documentation is of value for current and future informational purposes. Museum ownership is part of an object's provenance. Even in cases of total loss, a record of that consequence must be created and retained.

Deaccession Disclosure

It is recommended that museums provide public notification of deaccessions. This can happen before or after the fact. The secret and private removal of collections is to be avoided for several reasons. Museums purport to be about public benefit. In this capacity they tend to espouse concepts of accountability. Overt transparency is desirable for many operations, but especially those relating to collections.

Making deaccessions known in a transparent public manner will depend on various circumstances. Announcements could be required by a museum policy, or the action will become known during a removal process, as would happen when legal actions unfold.

Museum deaccession notifications can vary. The process itself often dictates how disclosure is accomplished. For example, if commercial deaccessioning by auction happens, declaring the museum as the consigner and noting how the proceeds will be used is easily shown in advertisements, catalogues, and other promotional materials. Similar information can be provided if an object is being sold through a private dealer. When an item is being given to another museum, the arrangement might be announced in a press alert. However items are removed, the action may be noted on the museum's website, in an annual report, by social media, or in newsletters or other communication vehicles.

Unless agreed to at the time of an acquisition, the idea of notifying the donor or a donor's heirs of a deaccessioned object is optional and entirely at the discretion of the removing museum. This should not be a categorical requirement but something done if a museum thinks it feasible and appropriate. The same applies for notifying donors, or heirs thereof, who gave money to purchase something that at a later time is deaccessioned. Offering to return a deaccessioned item to the original donor is ill advised (see chapter 5, Return).

Objects define museums. Much of what occurs in these institutions involves collections. From acquisitions to exhibitions to research to conservation, there is an emphasis on the things museums collect, study, preserve, and show. Deaccessioning can be misunderstood in those contexts. Consequently, when it comes to removing collections, full disclosure of the what, why, where, when, and how regarding the action is desirable.

How to fully disclose deaccessioning must be set in a museum's procedural documents well before the idea that objects might, in time, no longer be wanted in the permanent collection. The considerations reviewed in this chapter may not be directly relevant for every deaccession action, but the options must be recognized and when pertinent, officially approved as part of a policy process.

CHAPTER FIVE

DEACCESSIONING IMPLEMENTATION

Following official approval by a museum's board of trustees, the final act of deaccessioning takes place—implementing the departure of a collection item. It can happen in several ways. The removal can be done by sale, gift, exchange, demotion, destruction, return, or in compliance with a restriction. Often, museum collection management policies will describe and list options, and in a desired priority.

Whatever course of deaccession action takes place, it must be agreed upon in advance and recorded in appropriate museum records. Unless there are extenuating circumstances dictating otherwise, this information should be available to the public in a convenient and unobstructed manner. When a museum collection item moves from public ownership to private ownership, relevant arguments for the action need to be clearly documented by the removing organization.

Sale

There are three considerations to address when deaccessioning by selling:

- how to do it

- how to avoid contributing to illegitimate markets or illicit trade

- how to use the income

How to Sell Deaccessioned Collections

There has long been a commercial marketplace for most art and historic artifacts as well as many scientific specimens. Today it exists through brick-and-mortar businesses and on the Internet. A retail value for whatever a museum wants to deaccession can usually be determined. This is not to say markets are always and consistently robust or lucrative for every arcane area in which a museum collects.

Museums can sell objects themselves or work through private dealers, auction houses, or e-commerce companies. Generally, museums avoid being their own dealers. There are three reasons for this:

- Most have little ability to do this well.

- It might suggest everything a museum owns is for sale.

- It provides an "arms-length" distance from the commercial marketplace and helps protect against potential accusations of insider trading.

People working for museums may be familiar with the market for items represented in collections. However, they usually have neither the time nor expertise to get involved in selling with any impact and effectiveness. Moreover, they generally lack any infrastructure to do so. When it comes to selling, the best advice is: "Leave it to the experts." But as with so much else in life, chose the experts carefully.

Getting at least three bids from prospective qualified dealers is customary. Once selling has been selected as a deaccession route, realizing the most money on the transaction is usually paramount. Beware of pricey promises though. To get a museum's business, some dealers will suggest unrealistic sale results (that they cannot guarantee). Conversely, some dealers, especially auction houses, may encourage setting low sales estimated to encourage bidding. There is no right or wrong preference. I was once subjected to condescending scolding by a major auction house when I declined to use it to sell a deaccessioned piece of antique furniture because of the low estimate proposed. A competing, and the successful auction house, proposed a higher estimate. The piece sold well with the competing house.

An exception to museums commercially deaccessioning on their own happens when an object is sold to another museum. In those instances, maximizing a financial return might not be as important as assuring an item remains in the public sector and in a more appropriate repository. This sort of restricted sale can diminish retail options and possibly reduce income, but not always. Moreover, maximizing income may be a minor consideration. Regardless of the results, boards of trustees need to approve the choice and understand the consequences.

Museums can use private dealers, auction houses, targeted mail solicitations, or e-commerce outlets for selling collections. Deciding which option is best will depend on several factors, but usually a top consideration is realizing the maximum return. Commercial deaccessioning is one of the few times museums must venture into capitalism with unbridled verve. Are a museum's best interests served by selling an object in a dealer's shop, an auction gallery, online, or via some combination thereof? The considerations depend on several factors such as vendors' reputations, optimum sale schedules, the current state of a particular market, adherence to any deaccessioning restrictions regarding the sale of an item, and, as always, staff or trustee preferences and prejudices. Caution is advised regarding "personal" influences as the fact or perception of conflict of interest can be unfortunate for institutional reputations. Moreover, staff or trustee preference may be completely inapplicable when making market decisions.

Once commercial deaccessioning has been approved by a museum's board of trustees, seeking and getting the best vendor will require requesting sale proposals. It is usually easy to make up a select list of invitees. Some will respond favorably, and some will decline. This is a business transaction. Museums may want to set a minimum price received, but given the fluidity of certain markets and the oddity of certain things museums deaccession, that is not always possible. Dealers will have customary percentages they charge clients. Museums may enjoy discounts in this regard.

Sale proposals should contain a marketing plan. Which vendor appears to have the best and most realistic approach for getting the best price? Is there a no-fault time limit on agreements should a museum wish to change vendors? Issues of advertising, photography, conservation, transportation, handling, record keeping, storage, and other logistics need to be clearly spelled out. These can add to the cost of a sale and reduce profits. Finally, how will the museum's name be used in the sale? This is critical to an institution's reputation. Precise wording must be agreed upon before any contract is signed. The question of museum identity or anonymity when commercially deaccessioning is an institutional decision.

This might be already codified in collection management documents or decided on a case-by-case basis.

As noted repeatedly, it must be standard practice to recommend museums be completely transparent about deaccessioning, regardless of how it is accomplished. When selling items, a museum consigner may be listed in sales materials, by vendors, and in advertising or other promotions. These notices can be succinct or lengthy depending on the information a museum wants to communicate. It is customary to explain that an object(s) is being sold at the directive of the XYZ Museum's Board of Trustees. A reason might be noted, such as "to improve the quality of the permanent collections" or "dispose of a collection deemed inapplicable to the mission of the museum" or "as part of a process to redefine the museum's collection focus." If the museum adheres to generally accepted profession protocols about selling collections, there is a note explaining that the income from the sale will be used to fund collection acquisition and/ or the direct conservation of collections. Further explanations might be on a museum's website.

When the Western Reserve Historical Society, Cleveland, Ohio, deaccessioned nearly seventy automobiles from its Frederick C. Crawford Auto-Aviation Museum, it selected Sotheby's auction house. The preface to the fully illustrated catalogue outlined the organization's deaccession process and how the income would be used.

> The proceeds from this sale will be assigned, as specified in the Society's Collections Policy. Fifty percent will be placed in an acquisitions endowment fund, the income from which will allow the Society to purchase vehicles important to the collection and to fill gaps identified by the "blue-ribbon" committee. Fifty percent will go into the Crawford Museum's presently meager endowment, the income from which will be used to assure the proper care, maintenance and display of the automobile collection. (Barr and Sande 1990)

Deaccessioning has the potential to be a highly volatile media mess. Most of the time nothing untoward happens from a public relations standpoint. Nevertheless, any contradicting public opinions or misperceptions can lead to controversy. At the transaction level, the frequency of these is reduced if such action is understood to be hands-off and independent of the core mission of museums, which is to collect, preserve, and interpret valued collections for public benefit. Selling through an appropriately vetted third party helps guard against thoughts that everything a museum owns can be bought or that a deaccession hides some conflict of interest.

Public notice of commercial deaccessioning is especially easy to accomplish with auction houses and is why this sale option is favored by museums. Catalogues, as were shown in figure 2.1 (chapter 2), and online information can include the public pronouncements cited above. These provide both the sense and fact of transparency for museums. Institutional caveats can forbid trustee, staff, vendors, or others associated with the museum from bidding. The proscriptions help further reduce potential conflicts of interest. Suspicions will be raised if a museum sells something that is bought by an employee, trustee, volunteer, or even a relative, friend, or business associate of these folks. It is recommended that museums disqualify these people in some documented manner.

If required by a consigning museum, private dealers can adhere to the same notifications museums request of auction houses. The only difference is the final sale price of an object is usually not public record unless the museum notes it in hard copy or online information. Dealers never divulge the prices they realize for what they sell.

Whatever commercial deaccession option is selected, be it public, private, or intermuseum sales, the selling museum may want to consider imposing ownership restrictions. These can take many forms, but in the case of intermuseum sale one might require that the new museum give or sell it only to another museum should it be deaccessioned later. Museums hate restrictions about what they can do with their collections, but they happen and are still entered into.

Finally, regardless of how a museum chooses to commercially deaccession, it is strongly suggested nothing be sold on the museum's property. Public confusion will be certain as people think other things a museum owns are or could be for sale. A geographic and contractual distance literally helps separate the commerce of art and objects from the preservation of art and objects. This further explains why museums never, or rarely, sell antiques in their gift shops. They might offer art by living artists represented in their collections, but this is done in a controlled manner or on a small scale and seen as an obvious way to support artists.

How to Avoid Illegitimate Markets and Illicit Trade When Deaccessioning

Museums need to avoid unlawful, or even suspect, commercial options when they deaccession. Institutions should be watchful and aware of questionable retail trade practices and covert business operations. Being informed about existing and new national and international treaties relating to art, antiquities, and scientific specimens is essential. An examination of the nature of the item(s) being removed is required and what, if any, safeguards or laws might need to be abided by for disposal.

Being aware of illicit trade practices and illegitimate commercial or nefarious markets is an obvious important step in guarding against morally, ethically, or legally problematic deaccessioning. Objects important to certain Native American tribes may fall under NAGPRA covenants. Some natural history specimens might be protected by endangered species laws and treaties, be they local, national, or international. And a museum wishing to deaccession art entangled in repatriation disputes will have its plans compromised. Occasionally items requiring care can cross institutional disciplines and not be specific to any one sort of museum. Ivory offers a perfect example as it can be found in any of the three major museums types. Examples would include piano keys in history museums, sculpture in art museums, and natural history specimens in science museums.

The International Foundation for Art Research (IFAR, http://www.ifar.org) can provide assistance in knowing about laws and activities relating to legal and illegal matters of importance about museum collections as well as discussions underway in these realms. The organization can also help shed light on possible ownership questions about an object a museum wishes to deaccession. At the start, having the secure ownership and right to deaccession must be confirmed as part of the deaccession process. Over the years, on occasion purloined items have been innocently acquired by museums.

How to Use Income from Deaccession Sales

In the past few decades, American museum profession organizations have promulgated directives on how the income from the sale of deaccessioned collections should be used. These can be found in the codes of ethics of the American Alliance of Museums (AAM), the American Association for State and Local History (AASLH), and in regional museum association documents. The code of the AAM explains "in no event shall they be used for anything other than acquisition or direct care of collections" (AAM 2000). Museums increasingly embrace this principal in institutional collection management documents approved by governing bodies. These are rarely legally binding, however. Museum boards of trustees can have opinions and preferences that directly contradict or diverge from instructions listed by museum professional organizations and practitioners. For example, and as explained further, deciding what constitutes "direct care of collections" is subject to debate.

The prevailing standard of practice regarding deaccession income supports the idea that museum collections are not assembled or held for their monetary value. If or when collections become monetized and are seen simply as potential cash cows, their informational role evaporates. Museum collections may have a financial worth in the commercial sector, but that is irrelevant intellectually for museum purposes. Insurance policies for collections tend to be for blanket coverage, not individual content. Rarely are entire collections lost at once. Insurance coverage for individual objects usually happens when they are on loan from or to a museum. It may also apply for an individual object of exceptional monetary worth.

Rules about how sale proceeds should be used are set to avoid in principal and practice the collection-as-cookie-jar approach to financing operations. The hope is that museums will avoid selling collections to pay for debt, salaries, the utility bill, or capital projects having minimal if any direct contact with collections. That kind of behavior suggests museums are being poorly governed, and money realized from the sale of collections will hardly correct more fundamental faults. The income will only provide a temporary reprieve from obvious endemic failures at the governance level. The very survival of the museum becomes suspect.

Using the income from selling collections for new acquisitions is easily tracked and understood. Many museums set aside restricted accounts in their budgets or investments that only permit the money to be used to make collection purchases or for direct care of collections. Defining the "direct care of collections" is open to interpretation but usually means conservation measures involving physical actions to a collection item or items, or the immediate housing and preservation of these things. Some will argue that a new roof for a museum helps care for the collections contained therein, but that is usually too peripheral to be accepted as direct care. Similarly, paying for a conservator staff position can fall outside the realm of immediate specific collection care.

In 2016 the American Alliance of Museums issued a white paper presenting the findings of a panel organized to define the direct care of collections. Given the variety of museums in existence, from small art museums to large science museums to sprawling multibuilding history museums, the study recognizes an expansive rather than restrictive application of the concept. It includes a helpful chart for defining collection care priorities on a case-by-case, institution-by-institution basis (AAM 2016).

Codes of ethics may or may not correspond with specific laws and indeed often stand outside legal realms. They deal with matters of conduct that aspire to societal moral and behavioral standards, which may or may not be commonly shared. Generally, museum professional organization and institutional directives can be ignored if a trustee so wishes as long as the action does not violate any laws (as happens when a museum decides to deaccession by throwing in the trash old taxidermy mounts full of toxic materials or mishandling ivory that is subject to legal protections). Though there are customary preferences for how the proceeds from the sale of deaccessioned collections can be used, unless there are documented and binding restrictions on such income, museums can pretty much do as they wish with the money.

Museum policies dictating how collection sale income can be used are often meaningless when the museum is owned by a larger entity. Guidelines and other self-generated collection management documents may state that profits be used for acquisitions and/or direct collection care, but the authority that owns the museum can decide otherwise. For example, college and university museums are rarely independent of their owning entity. Perhaps the most alarming example of such realities involved the Rose Art Museum at Brandeis University when the board of trustees of the university decided to sell all or much of the most valuable art to cover the school's operating costs in 2009. A resulting controversy halted the plan, but it appeared the university trustees had the right to do what they wanted (Shea 2011).

Gift

Museums occasionally give deaccessioned items to a third party, which is almost always another museum. Intermuseum transfers can cause a win-win-win-win outcome. The beneficiaries are: the object, the deaccessioning museum, the receiving museum, and the public. Intermuseum gifting will mean the donating museum need not preserve something outside its mission or for which it cannot or does not want to devote resources. The receiving museum will welcome the object as mission relevant and worth caring for. The survival of the object will be assured for a longer period of time. The public will have access to it for the informational, emotional, and cultural reasons museum ownership champions.

Gifts to individuals (especially staff), commercial, and nonmuseum entities are generally avoided for obvious conflict-of-interest reasons. Nevertheless, unless restrictions are attached to their ownership, museums may have every legal right to do as they wish with deaccessioned material, including giving it to individuals, a business, or government office. Extreme caution is recommended in this regard.

When the Museum of the City of New York gave its retiring senior curator an accessioned six-volume set of vellum copies of *The Iconography of Manhattan Island*, the deaccessioning was approved by the board of trustees. The museum had seven copies (Author, personal knowledge).

Intermuseum transfers of collections are usually arranged through appropriate staff, but it must be approved and agreed to in a documented manner on institutional governance levels. Boards of trustees at both the giving and the receiving museums need to concur with the transfer in writing, and this information must be retained on file at both institutions. Such documentation will customarily be kept in collection management files, recorded in board meeting minutes, and held in museum administration offices. It is perfectly acceptable for the giving and receiving museums to set mutually agreed-upon, feasible restrictions to the gift.

How or if an intermuseum transfer of collections is made public will depend on the preferences of the giving and receiving museums. These are usually very good media stories; therefore, high-profile press coverage can be warranted.

A donor museum will be especially sensitive regarding how a gift is reported to the public. A museum's most important asset is its reputation.

Explaining the departure of collection items requires special care to avoid potential misunderstandings. It should be clear the deaccessioning in no way suggests the donor museum is failing in its mission. However, if a museum is in dire financial or other straits, it is paramount to avoid being disingenuous when it comes to announcing or justifying a deaccessioning. American museums are public stewards of physical legacies of art, history, and natural history for the general good. Fibbing rarely accrues to an institution's advantage.

How does a museum find a recipient for deaccessioned objects? There are several obvious ways, such as personal contact between professional colleagues, letters of inquiry soliciting interest, and advertisements placed in museum profession publications, relevant academic journals, or special interest periodicals of merit. Museums may carry deaccession notices on their websites.

Restrictions on gifts from one museum to another can include conservation caveats, exhibition directives, the exact wording of donor credit lines, research and informational access, preserving documents or archival materials related to an object, and assurances that the item will not be sold but transferred to another museum should the receiving museum no longer want or be able to keep it. This last instance may include returning an object to the donating museum. Restrictions can have time limits or are unlimited. Presumably there will be mechanisms for monitoring adherence. Consequences for violations should be agreed upon in advance.

Because museum boards of trustees are the designated fiduciaries of these institutions, they may be uncomfortable giving deaccessioned collections away rather than selling them. This is a philosophical discussion, the outcome of which depends on trustee whim, preference, experience, and governing practices. Certainly, a donation means a museum receives no money for the item. That may be inconsequential if preservation is imperative. The costs of such a transfer (and to be sure, there are always costs even if only indirect) may be borne by the giving and/or the receiving museum.

An exemplary intermuseum deaccession took place when the Museum of the City of New York gave to other museums a dressing room and bedroom it owned that were originally from the nineteenth-century Worsham-Rockefeller townhouse that once stood at 4 W. 54th Street, in Manhattan. The rooms are furnished in an ornate Aesthetic Period Orientalist style dating from the early 1880s. The Virginia Museum of Fine Arts received the bedroom, and the Metropolitan Museum of Art the dressing room (figure 5.1 shows the dressing room of the Warsham-Rockefeller House). The rooms had been on exhibit at the City museum for decades but were so inconveniently located as to often be closed to the public. They were clearly better suited to the two art museums that hold them now (Reagan 2008).

Exchange

At times museums may consider exchanging deaccessioned items. This is a variant of gifting because something is received in return for something removed. Matching participants takes place in much the same way as when one museum seeks another to receive a deaccession donation. It is not unusual for an exchange to be initiated between colleagues at different institutions, especially curators who might be more familiar with the holdings and interests of various museums.

Determining the equity of an intermuseum exchange will vary. One obvious way, often requested by trustees, is to compare the estimated current market price of whatever is being swapped. Are they of equal value? Does this matter?

The financial fairness of deaccession exchanges may be an inapplicable decision-making yardstick. Because museums rarely measure the importance of collections by their monetary worth, it must be the informational content that holds sway in these deliberations. An item of minimal retail value can be highly desired by a museum for aesthetic, scientific, or cultural documentary reasons. Both the removing and the receiving museums might need to acknowledge fiscal realities and be prepared to explain discrepancies in this regard. If appreciable differences in the "price" of exchanged objects is a negotiating issue, sometimes variances can be met by agreeing to include a dollar payment to balance the exchange.

Exchanges with individuals, art dealers, or antiques shops and other private participants may be legal, but these require extra special care and attention to avoid conflict-of-interest accusations. Moreover, museums should guard against being duped. The resulting transaction must appear

Figure 5.1.   Dressing Room, Warsham-Rockefeller House, 4 W. 54th Street, New York, USA. Deaccessioned by the Museum of the City of New York and given to the Metropolitan Museum of Art, New York, 2009. Photo by Steven Miller.

to have worked to the museum's clear and obvious advantage. Even when a museum comes out ahead, the transaction can be met with suspicion.

Most of the time few if any outsiders will be curious about or involved in deaccessioning. Yet this hardly diminishes the need for institutional behavior that is beyond reproach. When an object is owned on behalf of the public, as it is in a museum context, this fact is usually documented. The removal of a museum collection object, no matter the means, requires creating and retaining in writing the reason for and record of that action in collection management and other files. This is never more necessary than when something being deaccessioned will be lost to public ownership once sold into the private sector, as was done in 2008 by the National Academy of Design (see figure 5.2) and in 2015 by the Delaware Art Museum (see figure 5.3).

Considering the primary emphasis museums put on preserving collections, it can be argued that deaccessioning into the private sector is

Figure 5.2. *Scene on the Magdalene*, **by Frederic Edwin Church, 1854. One of two paintings deaccessioned by sale in 2008 by the National Academy of Design to pay for operating costs and capital improvements. Whereabouts unknown. Frederic Edwin Church [Public domain], via Wikimedia Commons. https://commons.wikimedia.org/wiki/File:Church.lrg.jpg.**

Figure 5.3. *Isabella and the Pot of Basil*, by William Holman Hunt, 1868. One of four artworks deaccessioned by sale by the Delaware Art Museum in 2015 to pay for operating costs and to retire construction debt. Whereabouts unknown. William Holman Hunt [Public domain], via Wikimedia Commons. https://commons.wikimedia.org/wiki/File:WHH_Isabella_Pot_of_Basil_DelArt.jpg.

tantamount to destroying what was once held in protective public custody. The act is an egregious failure of the stewardship imperative all museums espouse and relentlessly pursue.

Demotion

A museum may decide an accessioned item is worth keeping, but not as part of its permanent collection. There might be little mission relevance, content value, and/or preservation reason to hold an artwork, artifact, or scientific specimen as an accessioned object. Sometimes oddball accessioning occurs, as happens when office furniture gets inexplicably accessioned in some misguided approach to inventory everything a museum owns. Or, hands-on education props might inadvertently have accession numbers on them.

Collections deaccessioned but kept by a museum might become education props, office decor, or expendable research specimens. As with other forms of deaccessioning, pertinent documentation is required along with board approval and oversight. Records need to be examined to be certain there are no restrictions on what the museum can do with an item to be demoted.

Care must be exercised to avoid misunderstanding when what was once an accessioned object, subject to the protocols and protections of this status, is suddenly being used in a very different way. Perhaps an accessioned horse-drawn vehicle is deaccessioned to be used as it originally was. Also, accessioned numbers affixed to objects should be removed. Some sort of public explanation may be advisable regarding the "demotion" in a museum's ownership purpose.

Destruction

The destruction of a museum object as a form of deaccessioning is perhaps an unexpected application of the word. However, the outcome of such action is a form of collection removal. What was once in a museum is lost.

Deaccession by destruction can happen on purpose, by accident, natural disaster, human violence, neglect, or when a well-meaning attempt to preserve an object goes awry. Occasionally a collection object deaccessions itself, as might happen with early movie film that often has a high nitrate content and can self-combust when incorrectly stored. Or, munitions of the sort found in military museums can detonate.

There are times when a museum itself will deaccession something by destroying it. This might be the case with dangerous and/or mysterious chemicals and other toxic substances, or when something is so decomposed as to preclude any form of salvage. Or, when scientific research calls for destroying a specimen in the process of analysis.

Museums are devoted to preserving their collections for the long term. They do a good job when one considers the range and vast number of things responsibly held. Yet museums can be targets of assault as well as innocent victims of disaster. Guarding against harmful depredations is a constant responsibility. Sometimes even the most diligent protections fail or are impossible to sustain in the face of overwhelming odds.

Depending on why and/or how an object was destroyed, museum staff and governing bodies could try to avoid appearing complicit in deaccessioning by destruction. Nevertheless, keeping records of the result is important. Again, the role of the museum as science signifier, cultural memory bank, or explicator of artistic expression is essential. While losses by destruction happen, the fact of such acts and the outcomes must be documented for two reasons. For the most part, one hopes such actions might be avoidable in the future, and holding a record of the loss of museum collections once preserved will inform future generations.

Return

Deaccession by return involves giving an object to its donor, or a donor's heir(s), or an "original owner(s)," or to a designated political, national, or cultural group, or to a third party listed in a legal directive. Depending on why and how it is done, return options are either a free-will museum decision or one forced on it.

The idea of giving things back to donors or relatives might on the surface seem acceptable, but when examined there are drawbacks. If a donor realized a tax deduction for the value of his or her donation, the Internal Revenue Service may need to be alerted. Unless the gift had a restriction requiring the object be returned to the donor or a designee if no longer wanted, the museum is limiting its removal options when only considering this course of action. Locating the donor or heirs may be difficult, and it might be expensive to return the object. In the case of heirs, how will a museum know who is legitimate, much less deserving? Will a potential recipient want the object? What are the costs of returning the item? Will an individual benefit commercially from the professional storage, handling, exhibition, and publication afforded by museum ownership that assured the preservation of the object and perhaps increased its commercial value over time? Might there have been collusion in this regard, or, could there be the appearance of such? In other words, has a secret deal been arranged to permit a valued museum object to be transferred to an influential recipient who may be planning to sell it?

The return of deaccessioned items to an "original owner(s)" usually happens when something stolen is discovered in a museum collection. Statutes of limitations may not matter as museums can feel obligated to correct a perceived or actual wrong. To be sure, such motivation is laudable, but it is important to know the museum in question could also be a victim. Documenting an "original owner(s)" is obviously a requisite chore before giving any deaccessioned item to any recipient. As with art purloined by the Nazis during World War II that is found in museums, confirming where it came from can be fraught with confusion, debate, and mystery.

Most of what a museum owns is held legitimately and without suspicion regarding its acquisition. However, international or local sociopolitical changes can result in demands for museums to return objects of value to peoples of varying national, racial, gender, religious, economic, or ethnic identities. Museums may or may not be sympathetic to appeals and may or may not be legally obligated to respond.

An outside request for a museum to deaccession must rarely be agreed to without investigation. Research is required. Who is soliciting the museum? Is the demand valid and the case legitimate ethically, morally, or legally? Museums may want to consider the best interests of the object being sought. Will new owners be able to care for it as well as, or better than, the museum? Will the idea of public benefit be a consideration, and what is the relevant definition of *public*? Once a museum relinquishes an object to private ownership, it is no longer available to the general public. Will this matter? If so, what can be done about it?

Regardless of how, when, why, where, or to whom a deaccessioned item is returned, the action must be documented for museum files. Trustee approval, acknowledgment, or oversight is important to record even if the deaccession may have been forced on the museum.

Transfer to a Designated Government Authority

Once is a while, deaccessioning happens when a government agency takes ownership of something in a museum collection. There are few instances of this, but it is important to be aware of the possibility. One example would include the original design plans for Central Park, in New York City. These were in the custody of the Museum of the City of New York for decades (including while I was a curator of them, among the much larger picture collections). They consisted of panels created by Calvert Vaux and Frederick Law Olmstead, the mid-nineteenth-century designers of the park. Each panel had photo and drawing images of the ideas for various parts of the park. They had been accessioned. In time the City of New York recalled these, and they are now in its municipal archive.

The reasons for deaccessioning enumerated above may seem comprehensive and can be pursued without issue. Guess again. With the sometimes perilous nature of museum operations when combined with insecure governance structures and a beloved stature in the public's eye, debates will erupt about the wisdom of removing a collection item or two, or more. These will happen regardless of reason. Usually they unfold when a museum decides to sell items on the open market to pay for practical matters such as salaries, maintenance, or capital improvements.

References

AAM (American Alliance of Museums). 2000. "Code of Ethics for Museums. Collections." Adopted 1991; amended 2000. http://aam-us.org/resources/ethics-standards-and-best-practices/code-of-ethics.
————. 2016. "Direct Care of Collections: Ethics, Guidelines and Recommendations." American Alliance of Museums. April 2016. http://www.aam-us.org.

Barr, Douglas N., and Theodore Anton Sande. 1990. *Antique and Classic Automobiles from the Collection of the Frederick C. Crawford Auto-Aviation Museum of The Western Reserve Historical Society together with Property of Various Owners* . . . (Catalogue Preface). Sotheby's. New York, March 31, 1990.

Reagan, Gillian. 2008. "City Museum Disposes of Rockefeller Rooms." *Observer*, February 20, 2008. http://www.observer.com/2008/02/city-museum-disposes-of-rockefeller-rooms/.

Shea, Andrea. 2011. "After Controversy, Brandeis Brings Back the Rose Art Museum." *Boston Globe*, October 28, 2011. http://www.legacy.wbur.org/2011/10/28/rose-art-museum.

DEACCESSIONING CONTROVERSIES AND MORE

D espite the fact that deaccessioning is now a perfectly acceptable collection management option for museums, on occasion it can be a highly toxic subject with huge adverse public repercussions. The practice can be seen by some as violating public obligations museums assume in founding documents, by-laws, annual reports, and a host of media communiques. This is an unusual fact of life that every museum must be aware of and prepared for.

Deaccessioning and Controversy

Most museums are rarely the target of public controversy in any regular significant way. Day-to-day work is conducted without external debate. When museum activities are subjected to mainstream media attention in a negative way, they are usually about a staffing issue, financial mess, natural or civil calamity, misguided real estate venture, theft of property, collection ownership dispute, or deaccessioning. The last practice is a recurring subject for press coverage. "The concept of deaccessioning in the last 35 years has frequently been controversial as the profession has been ever more alert to issues of legal responsibilities, the public's expectations of museums, and ethics codes for institutions and individuals" (Morris and Moser 2010, 100).

Here are two motivations for why deaccessioning can cause a public kerfuffle: someone outside a museum takes issue with a specific collection removal decision, or the practice so contradicts the general understanding of what a particular museum is for that a group of individuals gets agitated and expresses loud disagreements. High-profile specific debates rarely emerge from within a particular museum or even the museum field itself.

The fact that persons outside the museum world could object to deaccessioning surfaced with a vengeance in the 1970s when the Metropolitan Museum of Art in New York City was "caught" selling paintings from its collection. John Canaday, art critic for the *New York Times*, lead a media alert exposing the undertaking (Canaday 1972). The Metropolitan Museum of Art issued a press release in June 1973 in response (appendix VI). Thomas Hoving, the museum's director who initiated and spearheaded the removal enterprise, tried to hide what he was doing. Predictably his obfuscations only energized press interest (Hess 1974).

Fortunately, the great deaccession debates that erupted five decades ago helped define the practice within the museum profession. Consequently, most institutions now follow what are considered generally accepted procedures recommended by various museum membership organizations. These are usually further encoded in individual museum policy documents.

When complaints arise about a museum deaccession, the museum in question needs to respond. I was the target of a pointed rebuke when I was director of the Bennington Museum in Bennington, Vermont. I recommended, and the museum board of trustees approved, the deaccession of a late-eighteenth-century chest-on-chest that had no relevance whatsoever for the museum. The chest was sold at auction with a catalogue entry noting that the piece was being removed at the direction of the Bennington Museum board of trustees and funds would be allocated to future acquisitions. Shortly after the sale a letter appeared in the local newspaper chastising the museum for the action (Dewey 2000). Perhaps, predictably, it offered no valid reason for the museum to keep the piece of furniture. A few days later, with trustee approval, I responded with a letter of explanation for the deaccession (Miller 2000). The complaint had no merit whatsoever, and the subject never came up again.

In 2016 the Toledo Museum of Art in Toledo, Ohio, was attacked for selling various antiquities from its collection. These included ceramics, bronzes, stone sculptures, and other objects from Egypt, Cyprus, Italy, and Greece. The governments of Egypt and Cyprus opposed the sale, as did a prominent art historian who grew up in Toledo. The museum followed customary deaccessioning procedures and explained these on its website and in press materials. The complaints were twofold: the loss of the pieces was a loss for the people of Toledo; and, the pieces would disappear into private ownership and thus no longer be part of the larger realm of publicly available antiquities (Gedert 2016).

The most common reason museums are criticized for deaccessioning unfolds when they do so to get operating funds. Such a maneuver signals a failure at the governance level of an institution. It indicates that bad financial decisions were made or are being made by a board of trustees. The action means that fiduciaries see collections as the contents of a cash "cookie jar" to be raided in times of economic duress. It heralds a fundraising failure at the board level. Trustees should be able to assure the fiscal health of the institutions for which they are responsible without threatening the treasures it holds in trust for present and future generations on behalf of past generations.

Two examples of controversies surrounding museums that engaged in selling collections in the recent past to cover operating costs involved the Delaware Art Museum and the National Academy Museum. Both were publicly pilloried for their actions (see figures 5.2 and 5.3). However, what the museums did was perfectly legal. Apparently, each had every right to dispose of the art as it wished. No ownership restrictions were in effect. Each publicly explained that its board of trustees had pursued a deliberative process of assessment and selection when choosing the art to be sold (Gascone 2015; Pogrebin 2010).

Another illustration of a deaccession controversy was unfolding as this book was being written. In 2017 the board of trustees of the Berkshire Museum, in Pittsfield, Massachusetts, decided to deaccession forty works of art by sale. The income, estimated to yield about $40 million, would be allocated for capital improvements and endowment. Protests from local residents and museum profession leaders and national organizations erupted immediately. There was even an antisale street demonstration in front of the museum (Moynihan 2017). The American Alliance of Museums' Code of Ethics says that proceeds from the sale of collections shall not "be used for anything other than acquisition or direct care of collection" (AAM 2000). The Association of Art Museum Directors' code includes an even narrower definition of when sales are permissible, stating, "A museum director shall not dispose of accessioned works of art in order to provide funds for purposes other than acquisitions of works of art for the collection" (AAMD 2010).

Recurring loud debates regarding deaccessioning and the residual consequences of the deaccession turmoil of the 1970s and 1980s have established two unofficial and informal monitoring sources. One is made up of people outside museums who are keenly interested in them and are watchful about how and when collections might be removed. The other monitor is museum staff who patrol themselves because they are very sensitive to potential and actual misunderstandings about deaccessioning.

Museums and museum professional organizations have formulated codes, directives, instructions, proscriptions, and more regarding deaccessioning. These actions have established the practice as largely acceptable when done in a certain way. Most museums abide by the advice. When they do not, controversy can arise.

It must be noted that to date, no museum embroiled in a deaccession debate has suffered egregious, quantitative, verifiable, long-term, publicly apparent adverse repercussions because of questionable collection removals. Moreover, most museum employees or trustees have never been held demonstrably accountable for deaccession actions they caused that ran counter to what is considered normal operating procedures within the mainstream museum profession. For example, no one associated with the Delaware Art Museum or the National Academy of Design lost a job or suffered any untoward legal actions. No one has gone to jail for wrongful deaccessioning.

Transparency and accountability are key managerial duties when museums are removing collections. Secretly deaccessioning things is unwise not only because the activity may cause alarm if "discovered" but also because museums increasingly must be open and above board in all transactions. As public stewards established to be of civic service, the actions of museums are subject to scrutiny on all levels of accountability. Having and adhering to professionally appropriate and governance mandated procedures helps explain all manner of things museums do. Setting, monitoring, and adhering to these can be effective public relations tools when it comes to collections.

Museums take different approaches to telling about or "announcing" deaccessions. Some are quiet; others make a big deal of it. Depending on the objects being removed and the timing and reasons for such removals, there will be varying levels of notifications regarding the nature and extent of any public pronouncements. For most private museums there are no required guidelines or directives, but some sort of overt mention of the action is recommended. A museum may want to simply record a deaccession in meeting minutes. Certainly, the action should be in collection management records.

Bringing a deaccession to wider attention can be easily done on websites, through emails, in newsletters, or at meetings open to members or general audiences. When something is being deaccessioned by transfer to another museum, this decision is often worthy of a special media release. This was certainly the case when Boscobel Restoration, Inc., in Garrison, New York, gave a c. 1850 painting of the United States Military Academy at West Point to the West Point Museum (see figure 3.2). The image was completely unrelated to the historic house's American Federal Period focus (see appendix III for the media alert for this gift).

Responding to Deaccession Controversy

As previously noted, the vast majority of collection disposals happen without public controversy, but from time to time debates can erupt. A museum must be prepared to respond if complaints surface about a deaccession decision. Deaccession grievances need to be countered by a qualified museum representative specifically designated for the task. Multiple respondents inevitably lead to confused and even contradictory explanations. A single and simple justification has to be provided, and it must be truthful, complete, and promptly delivered.

Describing a deaccession in a public manner should be a proactive rather than a reactive museum practice. In other words, announcing the action once it has been officially decided upon can help avoid external fault finding. The museum is more advantageously positioned for any possible protest. It sets the tone and presents an institutional agenda that may counter denunciations about covert or questionable methods of operation.

Deaccessioning announcements should succinctly list what is being removed, why, and how. If an item(s) is being sold, the use of the proceeds should be noted. When an object is being given to or exchanged with another museum, the outcome can be explained. If the deaccessioning is forced for legal reasons, that needs to be mentioned.

When a deaccession is implemented according to current museum profession practices, an institution will be prepared to answer any protests regardless of their origins or originators. The documentation and record of what was decided and why provide the baseline public relations material for explaining decisions. People can be assured that a responsible process was followed. This is not to say the deliberations museum employees and trustees engage in before removing collection items will always be understood or accepted by disgruntled opponents, but the measures can provide information for what was done.

Concluding Remarks

The concept of a place singularly designated to exclusively collect and save things in perpetuity for no immediate or long-term practical reasons is odd, to say the least. What is the point? Are the things worth saving forever?

The whole notion of museums is peculiar. Indeed, in the span of human existence they are new inventions. In the unlikely event they all disappeared tomorrow, would life as we know it collapse? No. There would be sadness in some circles and a lot of people would be unemployed, but most denizens of our globe would be completely unaffected and uncaring.

The impractical nature of museums is a philosophical question that has an impact on collection issues. In fact, it often causes collection issues. One of those issues is collection retention. Why, museum trustees in particular ask, do museums need to keep forever what they have acquired if there is no immediate or projected practical reason for doing so?

Americans are often described as an energetic bunch. The energy might be proactive or reactive, positive or negative in nature. Whether or not this is a national characteristic, it can offer a telling framework for discussing deaccessioning. "[M]useum philanthropy shares with every other modern American charitable cause the conviction that growth and progress are necessary in society and in charitable institutions; few public museums have been considered complete" (Fox 1995, 29). It is the nature of museums to shy away from stasis, at least in the United States. "A finished museum is a dead museum, and a dead museum is a useless museum" (Fox 1995, 34).

For museums, the agitation to change has had a serious impact on collections. Previously these holdings were safe from potential trustee and staff disruptions, especially regarding disposals. There was an unspoken mantra: museums collected; museums had collections; museums never got rid of collections. The secure isolation of collections is a thing of the past. Consequently, they are increasingly subject to removal suggestions. This notion will not abate. On the contrary, as museums relentlessly acquire items, collection magnitude will become a major challenge for institutions of all sizes.

Museums are encouraged to be transparent and forthright about how decisions are made when it comes to all manner of operations. This is especially important for collection duties. It is a long overdue development. When it comes to deaccessioning, the practice is laudable.

The human and natural universe is awash with things. As museums decide what is important to collect in perpetuity, they must also assess existing collections in consideration of this lofty goal. A growing conversation by those responsible for museums will relentlessly question once-sacred beliefs regarding the very idea of a permanent collection.

References

AAM (American Alliance of Museums). 2000. "Code of Ethics for Museums. Collections." Adopted 1991; amended 2000. http://aam-us.org/resources/ethics-standards-and-best-practices/code-of-ethics.

AAMD (American Association of Museum Directors). 2010. "AAMD Policy on Deaccessioning." June 9, 2010; amended by Board on October 4, 2010. https://aamd.org/sites/default/files/document/AAMD%20Policy%20on%20Deaccessioning%20website_0.pdf.

Canaday, Joan. 1972. "Very Quiet and Very Dangerous." *New York Times*, February 27. http://www.nytimes.com/1972/02/27/archives/very-quiet-and-very-dangerous.html.

Dewey, Charles. 2000. "Museum's Policy of Selling Pieces Is Disturbing" (Letter to the Editor). *Bennington Banner*, January 29, 14.

Fox, Daniel M. 1995. *Engines of Culture: Philanthropy and Art Museums*. New Brunswick, NJ: Transaction Publishers.

Gascone, Sarah. 2015. "Delaware Art Museum Sells Off Paintings by Winslow Homer and Andrew Wyeth." *Artnet News*, June 30. https://news.artnet.com/market/delaware-art-museum-deaccession-313082.

Gedert, Roberta. 2016. "Controversial Auctioning of Artifacts Ends; Rare Toledo Pieces Produce Revenue for New Purchases." *The Blade*, October 26.

http://www.toledoblade.com/Art/2016/10/27/Controversial-auctioning-of
-Toledo-Museum-of-Art-artifacts-ends.html.

Hess, John L. 1974. *The Grand Acquisitors.* New York: Houghton Mifflin.

Miller, Steven. 2000. "Response to Mr. Dewey's Letter about Our Museum"
(Letter to the Editor). *Bennington Banner*, February 3, 12.

Morris, Martha, updated by Antonia Moser. 2010. "Chapter 31. Deaccessioning." In *Museum Registration Methods*, 5th edition, ed. Rebecca A. Buck
and Jean Allman Gilmore, 100–7. Arlington, VA: American Association of
Museums.

Moynihan, Colin. 2017. "Berkshire Museum's Planned Sale of Art Draws Oppo-
sition." *New York Times*, July 25. https://www.nytimes.com/2017/07/25/
arts/design/berkshire-museum-art-auction-criticized.html.

Pogrebin, Robin. 2010. "Sanctions Are Ending for Museum." *New York Times*,
October 18. http://www.nytimes.com/2010/10/19/arts/design/19sanctions.
html.

APPENDIX I

AAMD Policy on Deaccessioning

June 9, 2010
Amended 10/2015—*Amended by Board on 10/2015*

AAMD Mission Statement

The Association of Art Museum Directors promotes the vital role of art museums throughout North America and advances the profession by cultivating leadership and communicating standards of excellence in museum practice.

Preamble

Deaccessioning is defined as the process by which a work of art or other object (collectively, a "work"), wholly or in part, is permanently removed from a museum's collection. Disposal is defined as the transfer of ownership by the museum after a work has been deaccessioned; in the case of false or fraudulent works, or works that have been irreparably damaged or cannot practically be restored, removal from the collection and disposition is determined by the museum and may include destruction of the work.

AAMD recognizes the unique challenges museums face in managing and developing collections largely built through gift and bequest by private donors. Most art museums continue to build and shape their collections over time to realize more fully and effectively their mission. Acquisitions to or deaccessions from the museum's collection must be guided by well-defined written collecting goals and acquisition and deaccession principles, procedures, and processes approved by a museum's Board of Trustees or governing body. These goals, principles, procedures, and processes must conform to AAMD's *Professional Practices in Art Museums* and AAMD's Policy on Deaccessioning.*

Deaccession decisions must be made with great thoughtfulness, care, and prudence. Expressions of donor intent should always be respected in deaccession decisions and the interests of the public, for whose benefit collections are maintained, must always be foremost in making deaccession decisions.

Policy Statement

A. AAMD requires member museums[†] to develop clear written collections management policies including written collection goals and acquisition and deaccession principles, procedures, and processes, as well as those that address preservation, conservation, and collection care.[‡]

B. AAMD encourages member museums to accept into the collection only gifts of works that support the mission of the institution and to be thoughtful about accepting gifts of works with restrictions.

C. Member museums must comply with all applicable laws, including, if applicable to the AAMD member museum, the filing of required Internal Revenue Service forms, in deaccessioning and disposing of works from the collection.

D. Member museums should not capitalize or collateralize collections or recognize as revenue the value of donated works. In 1992, following proceedings involving the museum profession, the Financial Accounting Standards Board (FASB) established standards regarding how museums (and other entities) that are subject to FASB[§] may account for their collections assuming certain conditions are met. As a result, in 1993, FASB issued Statement No. 116. The Statement, as amended, provides that contributions of works of art, historical treasures, and similar assets need not be recognized as revenue or capitalized if the donated items are added to collections that are (a) held for public exhibition, education, or research in furtherance of public service; (b) protected, kept unencumbered, cared for, and preserved; and (c) subject to an organizational policy that requires the proceeds from sales of collection items to be used to acquire other items for the collection. *Amended by Board on 10/2015*

E. When recommending a work to the museum's Board of Trustees for deaccessioning, a member museum's staff should provide thorough research on prior ownership history, an explanation of expressed donor intent, if any, current scholarly evaluation, and relevance to the existing collection and future collecting goals.

F. A member museum should publish on its website within a reasonable period of time works that have been deaccessioned and disposed of.

Application
I. Purpose of Deaccessioning and Disposal

A. Deaccessioning is a legitimate part of the formation and care of collections and, if practiced, should be done in order to refine and improve the quality and appropriateness of the collections, the better to serve the museum's mission.

B. Funds received from the disposal of a deaccessioned work shall not be used for operations or capital expenses. Such funds, including any earnings and appreciation thereon, may be used only for the acquisition of works in a manner consistent with the museum's policy on the use of restricted acquisition funds. In order to account properly for their use, AAMD recommends that such funds, including any earnings and appreciation, be tracked separate from other acquisition funds. *Amended by Board on 10/2015*

II. Criteria for Deaccessioning and Disposal

There are a number of reasons why deaccessioning might be contemplated. Primary among these are:

A. The work is of poor quality and lacks value for exhibition or study purposes. *Amended by Board on 10/2015*

B. The work is a duplicate that has no value as part of a series.

C. The museum's possession of the work may not be consistent with applicable law, e.g., the work may have been stolen or illegally imported in violation of applicable laws of the jurisdiction in which the museum is located or the work may be subject to other legal claims.

D. The authenticity or attribution of the work is determined to be false or fraudulent and the object lacks sufficient aesthetic merit or art historical importance to warrant retention. In disposing of or retaining a presumed forgery, the museum shall consider all related ethical issues including the consequences of returning the work to the market.

E. The physical condition of the work is so poor that restoration is not practicable or would compromise the work's integrity or the artist's intent. Works damaged beyond reasonable repair that are not of use for study or teaching purposes may be destroyed.

F. The work is no longer consistent with the mission or collecting goals of the museum. The Board of Trustees or governing body of the museum must exercise great care in revising a museum's mission or reformulating collecting goals.

G. The work is being sold as part of the museum's effort to refine and improve its collections, in keeping with the collecting goals reviewed and approved by the museum's Board of Trustees or governing body.

H. The museum is unable to care adequately for the work because of the work's particular requirements for storage or display or its continuing need for special treatment. *Amended by Board on 10/2015*

III. Authority and Process

A. Deaccessioning and disposal must comply with all applicable laws of the jurisdiction in which the museum is located and must observe any terms or obligations that pertain to the acquisition of the work by the museum.

B. The final authority for the deaccessioning and disposal of works rests with the Board of Trustees or governing body or its designee.

C. The process of deaccessioning and disposal must be initiated by the appropriate professional staff and any recommendations, with full justification, presented to the director, who will review the facts and circumstances of the proposed deaccession and disposal. As part of this process, the staff must undertake a thorough review of all records to determine donor intent, clear title, donor restrictions, and current market value. If the director determines that deaccessioning is appropriate, the proposal shall be presented to the Board of Trustees or governing body or its designee in accordance with the steps outlined in the museum's collection policy with regard to deaccessioning.

1. The director shall exercise care to assure that the recommendations are based on authoritative expertise. *Amended by Board on 10/2015*

2. Third-party review and appraisal may be considered in the case of objects of substantial value.

3. In the case of work(s) by a living artist, special considerations may apply.

D. The timing and method of disposal should be consistent with the museum's collection policy. Attention must be given to transparency throughout the process.

E. No member of a museum's board, staff, or anyone whose association with the museum might give them an advantage in acquiring the work, shall be permitted *Amended by Board on 10/2015* to acquire directly or indirectly a work deaccessioned, wholly or in part, by the museum, or otherwise benefit from its sale or trade; provided, however, that the foregoing shall not apply to a sale by a museum of its interest in a work to one or more of the co-owners of such work.

F. If a museum is proposing to dispose of less than all of its interest (sometimes known as fractional deaccessioning) in a deaccessioned work (unless the interest to be retained is insubstantial[4]), the disposal should only be made to an organization** or organizations that are open to the public. Examples of the foregoing are provided on Annex A.

IV. Selection of Methods of Disposal

The following may be taken into account in selecting a method of disposal:

A. Preferred methods of disposal are sale or transfer to, or exchange with another public institution, sale through publicly advertised auction, and sale or exchange to or through a reputable, established dealer. Every reasonable effort should be taken to identify and evaluate the various advantages and yields available through different means of disposal. *Amended by Board on 10/2015*

B. In the case of a work of art by a living artist, consideration may be given to an exchange with the artist.

C. While it is understood that museums must fulfill their fiduciary responsibilities and act in the museum's best interests, museums may give consideration to keeping a deaccessioned work in the public domain. *Amended by Board on 10/2015*

V. Interests of Donors and Living Artists/Notifications

A. Museums should notify the donor of a work, when practicable, under consideration for deaccessioning and disposal. Circumstances may warrant extending similar courtesy to the heirs of a donor.

B. When a work by a living artist is deaccessioned, consideration must be given to notifying the artist.

VI. Documentation

When a work is deaccessioned, all electronic and paper records must be updated. Prior to disposal, an image should be taken of the work and retained in the museum's records. As works are disposed of, the method of disposition, including possible consignee, new owner, sale price, and location, if known, should be recorded according to the museum's collection management policy.

VII. Special Circumstances

AAMD recognizes that part of the mandate of a contemporary arts organization is to expand the definition of what constitutes a work of art, as well as to question traditional exhibition practices. Therefore, if the organization's written policy provides for the sale of deaccessioned works, the funds derived from such sales may in exceptional cases be used for purposes analogous to the purchase or commission of works of art, specifically the creation of new works, including some that may not be collectible. Expenditure of these funds for operations or capital expenses is precluded. *Amended by Board on 10/2015*

VIII. Sanctions

In the event an AAMD member or museum violates one or more of the provisions of this policy, the member may be subject to censure, suspension, and/or expulsion; and the museum may be subject to censure and/or sanctions in accordance with the relevant provisions of the code of ethics of the AAMD, which have been amended consistent with the following: *Amended by Board on 10/2015*

Infractions by any art museum may expose that institution to censure and/or sanctions, as determined by the Board of Trustees of the AAMD (the "Board"), that may, in the case of sanctions, include, without limitation, suspension of loans and shared exhibitions between the sanctioned museum and museums of which the AAMD members are directors.

Prior to censuring or recommending suspension or expulsion of a member or censuring or issuing any sanction against an art museum, the Board shall provide to the director or museum in question the opportunity to be heard and to explain the reason for the actions considered for censure, suspension, expulsion, or sanction; such presentation to be by the affected director unless otherwise determined by the Board or, in the case of a museum, the director or any member of the board of trustees or governing board of the museum, as determined by the museum with the concurrence of the Board. If the Board determines to censure or recommend suspension or expulsion of a member or to censure or sanction a museum, the Board shall, contemporaneously with the issuance of a censure or sanctions or the recommendation of suspension or expulsion, determine and advise the affected director or museum of the process that may be followed, as the case may require, to allow the censure to be rescinded or modified, the suspension to be lifted, the expulsion to not bar a subsequent application for admission or the sanction to be lifted. *Amended by Board on 10/2015*

In the event that the museum is not a legal entity but rather part of an entity or controlled by another entity, any censure or sanction may be issued against the museum, the entity of which the museum is a part, the entity controlling the museum, or, as applicable, all of the foregoing as the Board shall determine (collectively, a "museum").

IX. Process for Review of Sanctions

The process to be followed for a censure against a member or museum to be rescinded, a sanction against a museum to be modified or rescinded, a suspension of a member to be lifted, or an expulsion of a member to not bar a subsequent application for admission, shall be as follows.

A. Censured Member or Museum. If a censure has been issued against a member or museum, the Board may, at any time, on its own motion, or at the written request of the affected member or museum, after due deliberation, rescind, modify, or declare as no longer in effect any censure.

B. Suspended Member. If a member has been suspended from membership in good standing with the AAMD, such suspension shall remain in place for the period, if any, specified in the suspension as issued or subsequently modified. If no period is indicated, the suspension shall remain in place indefinitely. Prior to the expiration of a stated suspension period, the Board should determine if the suspension should be extended and, if so, if the suspension should be modified. For suspensions with an indefinite period, the Board should review the suspension not less than every two years from the inception date of the suspension and determine if the suspension should be modified, terminated, or remain in place. *Amended by Board on 10/2015*

At any time, the suspended member may deliver a request in writing, addressed to the Executive Director of the AAMD, asking that the Board lift the suspension and reinstate the member as a member in good standing. In order to be considered by the Board, the request should (i) articulate the reasons that the suspension should be lifted, (ii) affirm that there are no continuing adverse effects caused by the action or actions of the member that resulted in the issuance of the suspension in the first instance, (iii) affirm that the suspended member has ceased practicing the sanctioned behavior and will not practice the sanctioned behavior in the future, and (iv) confirm that the member meets all of the qualifications for reinstatement as a member in good standing of the AAMD. Generally speaking, the Board shall be guided by the following considerations with respect to the lifting of suspension of a member: (a) if the violation that resulted in the suspension or the negative effects of such violation are not continuing at the time of the request and (b) the member has agreed to be vigilant in using his or her best efforts to avoid or prevent any future violation of the provisions of the Professional Practices in Art Museums. *Amended by Board on 10/2015*

C. Expelled Member. If a former member has been expelled from membership, after a period of five years has elapsed since the issuance of the expulsion, that person may deliver a request in writing, addressed to the Executive Director of the AAMD, requesting that the Board permit the former member to submit a subsequent application for admission as a member in good standing with the AAMD. In order to be considered by the Board, the request should articulate the reasons for seeking permission to submit a subsequent application for admission and, in connection therewith, shall confirm that there are no continuing adverse effects caused by the action or actions that resulted in the expulsion in the first instance and that the expelled member has ceased practicing the sanctioned behavior and will not practice the sanctioned behavior in the future. Generally speaking, the Board shall be guided but not bound by the following considerations with respect to permitting the submission of a subsequent application for admission as a member: (a) if the violation that resulted in the expulsion or the negative effects of such violation are not continuing at the time of the request or personal appearance and (b) the former member has agreed to be vigilant in using his or her best efforts to avoid or prevent any future violation of the provisions of the Professional Practices in Art Museums.

D. Sanctioned Art Museum. If a sanction has been issued against an art museum, such sanction shall remain in place for the period, if any, specified in the sanction as issued or subsequently modified. If no period is indicated, the sanction shall remain in place indefinitely. Prior to the expiration of a stated sanction period, the Board should determine if the sanction should be extended and, if so, if the sanction should be modified. For sanctions with an indefinite period, the Board should review the sanction not less than every five years from the inception date of the sanction and determine if the sanction should be modified, suspended, terminated, or remain in place. *Amended by Board on 10/2015*

At any time, an authorized representative of the art museum (e.g., the director or any member of the board of trustees or governing board of the museum) may deliver a written request to the Executive Director of the AAMD, asking that the Board modify, suspend, or terminate the sanction. The request should articulate the specific steps that the museum has taken to ameliorate the conduct which gave rise to the sanctions. Generally speaking, the Board shall be guided but not be bound by the following considerations with respect to modifying, suspending, or terminating sanctions against a museum: (a) if the representative has introduced new facts not previously disclosed that are of such significance that they would, in the view of the Board, cause the Board to change its initial determination of the imposition of the sanction or (b) if the museum has ceased the activity that gave rise to the sanctions, has affirmed that it will not practice the sanctioned conduct in the future, and has demonstrated that it has taken the appropriate steps to avoid a repetition of the conduct that gave rise to the sanctions. *Amended by Board on 10/2015*

E. General. 1. Board Review of Petitions; Delegation of Authority. The Board may delegate to (i) a committee of the Board, or (ii) the Executive Director acting in conjunction with the President, (A) the authority to review and make recommendations to the Board with respect to any requests referenced herein, (B) to determine, in the Board's stead, whether any request for personal appearance should be granted and, (C) if granted, to attend in the Board's stead, any such personal appearance.

2. Personal Appearance. Any request made in accordance with this Section IX may include a request to make a personal appearance before the Board to afford the requesting member, former member, or museum to explain his, her, or its position regarding the matters addressed in the request; provided, however, that the sole purpose of any such personal appearance shall be to elucidate the points made in the request and in no event shall such personal appearance take the place of the request itself. The Board or its delegees shall review any such request for personal appearance and determine, in its sole discretion, whether or not to grant a personal appearance. If a personal appearance is permitted, the person to appear shall be given notice and a mutually convenient time shall be scheduled by the Executive Director for the person to personally appear to present the request. In the case of a museum, the director or any member of the board of trustees or governing board of the museum may appear on the museum's behalf if a request for a personal appearance is made and granted. *Amended by Board on 10/2015*

3. Counsel. At any personal appearance under Subsection E(2) above, the person to appear may be accompanied by counsel at such person's expense; provided that ten (10) days' advance notice of the appearance of counsel at such personal appearance is provided to the Executive Director. If properly noticed, such counsel may accompany the person making the personal appearance; however, unless the Board otherwise determines, only the person requesting the personal appearance will be permitted to address the Board or its delegees to articulate his, her, or its position with respect to the request during the personal appearance.

4. Board Determination; Timing. Normally, the Board will issue its

determination with respect to the requests properly submitted hereunder within 120 days after the regularly scheduled Board meeting next following (i) the delivery of the written request to the Executive Director or, in the event of a personal appearance, (ii) the date of the personal appearance. Written notice of the determination of the Board will be provided in writing to the person making the request. The decision to rescind a censure, the issuance or subsequent review of any censure, sanction, suspension, or expulsion or rescind, suspend, or modify a sanction, lift a suspension, or allow an expulsion not to bar a subsequent application for admission and the imposition of any conditions or limitations as to any of the foregoing are solely within the discretion of the Board, and the Board may take into account any facts it deems relevant to its decision and may conduct, or not conduct, any investigation it may deem relevant. Any determination of the Board with respect to a request delivered hereunder will be final and non-appealable. *Amended by Board on 10/2015*

5. No Third Parties. Professional Practices in Art Museums and its Appendices, as well as Guidelines and Policies of the AAMD, are solely for the benefit of AAMD Members, and no third party shall have any right to enforce or demand that the AAMD enforce any provision of any of the foregoing.

X. University and College Museums

University and college museums play a significant role in acquiring, preserving, and presenting collections. While the primary focus of the university or college is education, it must also adhere to professional standards and ethics when operating a museum.

A. The director is responsible for the development and implementation of policy related to all aspects of the museum's collections, including acquisition, deaccessioning, and disposal, preservation, conservation, and exhibition, as well as scholarly research and interpretation. The director is responsible for ensuring that the university or college is aware of its ethical responsibilities to the art museum's collection, including issues around its deaccessioning, use, and the physical conditions under which it is maintained. *Amended by Board on 10/2015*

B. Deaccessioning and disposal from the collection must result from clear museum policies that are in keeping with the AAMD's Professional

Practices (see also the section on The Collection and Appendix B). Deaccessioning and disposal from the art museum's collection must never be for the purpose of providing financial support or benefit for other goals of the university or college or its foundation. In no event should the funds received from disposal of a deaccessioned work be used for operations or capital expenditures. *Amended by Board on 10/2015*

C. Policies developed by the director with regard to acquisition and deaccession should be adopted or ratified by the central governing authority of the university or college.

Used with permission of the Association of Art Museum Directors.

Notes

*Canadian and Mexican member museums should follow applicable legal restrictions and policies of national associations and, to the extent not inconsistent with either of the foregoing, AAMD's *Professional Practices in Art Museums* and AAMD's Policy on Deaccessioning. *Amended by Board on 10/2015*

†"Member museums" means those museums whose director is a member of the AAMD.

‡Museums that follow other accounting rules, such as those of the Government Accounting Standards Board (GASB), or are subject to contrary legal restrictions, may be required to treat collections for financial statement purposes in a different manner, but museums still should not collateralize their collections.

§For example, rights of reproduction or the right to borrow the work.

**"Organization" means a museum or institution exempt from federal income tax and classified as a public charity or a private operating foundation (or a substantially similar organization in Canada or Mexico) or governmental entity or agency.

APPENDIX II

New York State Museum:
A Sample Collections Management Policy

A Collection Management Policy is required of every New York educational corporation that owns or holds collections, intends to own or hold collections, or has owning or holding collections as one of its charter purposes.

All Collection Management Policies must address four major issues:

1) Acquisition—the criteria that are used for determining what items may be included in the collections and the procedures that are used by the corporation for accepting items for the collections.

2) Preservation—the procedures and parameters to be used to ensure the adequate care of collections materials.

3) Access—the procedures by which the materials in the collections will be made available to persons with legitimate reasons to access them.

4) Deaccession—the criteria that are used for determining what items may be removed from the collections and the procedures for removing those items and the use of any funds therefrom derived.

Attached is a suggested model policy which your organization may adopt in its entirety or modify to meet your particular needs. Your modifications must remain within the scope of accepted museological and historical agency practice, and conform to Regents rules on collections management. We can also provide reprints of articles to help your organization in the development of a policy. For additional help, we suggest that you examine the policies of similar organizations in your geographical area or subject field so that you can get a sense of how other organizations have addressed their collection management concerns. Lastly, regional and statewide museum and historical agency associations occasionally sponsor workshops and discussions about collection management, which we urge you to attend.

Once your organization has adopted a policy, or modified or revised an existing policy, you must send a copy of the new policy to our office at:

Chartering Program New York State Education Department 10A33 Cultural Education Center Albany NY 12230 **Phone:** (518) 474–5976 **E-mail:** charters@nysed.gov

Please call us if you have questions about collection management policies or these requirements.

This model policy was last revised September 1, 2012

Name of Educational Corporation (*enter below*):

Collection Management Policy

Purpose: To establish rules, guidelines, and procedures for the acquisition, care, preservation, public access, and deaccessioning of items in the collections of the above-named educational corporation, hereinafter referred to in this document as the "Corporation."

I. Collections Committee

The Board of Trustees of the Corporation shall establish a Collections Committee. Pursuant to the Corporation's By-Laws, the President shall appoint the members and chair of this Committee. The Committee shall recommend items for accession to and deaccession from the collections of the Corporation.

The Collections Committee shall include in its deliberations, whenever deemed necessary, the advice of professionals with the goal of making well-considered and timely recommendations to the Board of Trustees.

The final decision to accession, to acquire without accessioning, or to deaccession items to or from the collections of the Corporation shall rest with the Board of Trustees.

II. Acquisition

A. Scope. The Corporation collects printed and manuscript materials, maps, photographs, motion picture film, video and audio tapes (oral histories), paintings, artifacts, and other items which have been created or used in the following location, community, or geographical area, or are relevant to the following subject area (*fill in this section*):

B. Guidelines. Acquisitions to the Corporation's collections by purchase, loan, gift, bequest, or other means shall accord with the following rules:

1. The owner must have clear title and must sign a deed of gift transferring title to the Corporation. In the case of a bequest, the donor must also have had clear title.

2. A transfer or ownership file containing gift agreements and other proofs of the Corporation's legal ownership of acquisitions shall be maintained.

3. Acquisitions by purchase shall not exceed the annual budget for such purchases unless additional proper financing has been arranged.

4. No acquisition shall be appraised by a trustee, staff member, or any other person closely associated with either. (See U.S. Tax Reform Act of 1984 and Internal Revenue Service regulations relating to the act.)

5. The Corporation must be capable of housing and caring for the proposed acquisition according to generally accepted professional standards.

6. Proposed acquisitions shall be free of donor-imposed restrictions unless such restrictions are agreed to by the Collections Committee and the Board of Trustees.

7. Acquisitions approved by the Board of Trustees for accessioning shall be promptly accessioned upon receipt and acceptance under a system approved by the Collections Committee and the Board of Trustees.

8. Donors and prospective donors, whenever deemed appropriate, should be asked by the Collections Committee whether they would be willing to provide funds for the full or partial cost of accessioning and subsequent maintenance of materials gifted to the Corporation. Willingness or unwillingness to provide such funds should usually not be a determining factor in the Board of Trustees' decision to accept or reject a gift for accessioning.

III. Care and Preservation

The Corporation realizes its obligation to protect its collections which are held in the public trust. Therefore, the Corporation shall act to the best of its ability, according to the following guidelines:

A. A stable environment for items in storage or on display shall be maintained by protecting them from excessive light, heat, humidity, and dust. The environmental needs of different materials shall be considered.

B. All materials shall be protected against theft, fire, and other disasters by a security system and by a written disaster plan.

C. When possible, paper materials shall be copied on microfilm, photocopied on acid-free paper, or otherwise made redundant and stored in a separate location.

D. When deemed necessary, conservation of materials shall be undertaken with the advice of a trained conservator.

E. Records shall be kept using appropriate forms for documentation: i.e., temporary receipt form, deed of gift, accession forms, relevant correspondence, conservation reports, and deaccession records.

F. Inventories and location records shall be kept up to date to facilitate public access and to prevent loss.

IV. Public Access

The Corporation shall make research materials in its possession available to legitimate researchers with legitimate justification, but with the following stipulations:

A. Inventories, relevant files, and the assistance of a staff member or trained volunteer shall be available to users.

B. A registration form listing rules for usage shall be read, filled out, and signed by all researchers.

C. The Corporation may limit the use of fragile or usually valuable materials.

D. Hours of operation may be by designated hours or by appointment, depending on the availability of staff or trained volunteers.

E. Photographic and xerographic reproduction:

1. A Request for Copies form containing a notice of copyright restriction shall be signed by each user before copies are made.

2. Copies may not be used "for any purpose other than private study, scholarship or research." (United States Copyright Law, Title 17)

3. Reproduction by the corporation in no way transfers either copyright or property rights, nor does it constitute permission to publish or to display materials.

4. All prices for copying shall be determined by the Board of Trustees.

5. In some cases, the Corporation may refuse to allow copies to be

made because of the physical condition of the materials, restrictions imposed by the donor, copyright law, or right-to-privacy statutes.

F. A fee may be charged for research work done to meet requests: the amount shall be set by the Board of Trustees.

G. The Corporation may refuse access to an individual researcher who has demonstrated such carelessness or deliberate destructiveness as to endanger the safety of the materials.

In addition, the Corporation is committed to bringing to the public information culled from its documents, photographs, artifacts, and oral histories by presenting public programs, including slide shows, live acts, videos and films; mounting exhibits; and publishing newsletters, pamphlets, checklists, and guides to the collections whenever possible.

V. Deaccession

No accessioned object or collection shall be removed from the Corporation's auspices except in conformity with the following rules:

A. A deaccession recommendation shall be prepared by the Collections Committee and approved by the Board of Trustees. Whenever deemed necessary, professional advice shall be sought before an item is deaccessioned.

B. The decision to deaccession should be cautious and deliberate and follow generally accepted museological standards. One of the following criteria must be met:

1. The item is inconsistent with the mission of the institution as set forth in its mission statement;
2. The item has failed to retain its identity;
3. The item is redundant;
4. The item's preservation and conservation needs are beyond the capacity of the institution to provide;
5. The item is deaccessioned to accomplish refinement of collections;
6. It has been established that the item is inauthentic;
7. The institution is repatriating the item or returning the item to its rightful owner;
8. The institution is returning the item to the donor, or the

donor's heirs or assigns, to fulfill donor restrictions relating to the item which the institution is no longer able to meet;

9. The item presents a hazard to people or other collection items; and/or

10. The item has been lost or stolen and has not been recovered.

C. No donated material shall be deaccessioned for two years after the date of its acquisition. (See U.S. Tax Reform Act of 1984 and Internal Revenue Service regulations relating to the act.)

D. Ensure that collections or any individual part thereof and the proceeds derived therefrom shall not be used as collateral for a loan.

E. Ensure that collections shall not be capitalized.

F. A complete record of deaccessions shall be kept. A copy of this record shall be retained permanently.

G. Proceeds derived from the deaccessioning of any property from the collection of the Corporation shall be placed either in a temporarily restricted fund to be used only for the acquisition, preservation, protection, or care of collections, or in a permanently restricted fund the earnings of which shall be used only for the acquisition, preservation, protection, or care of collections. In no event shall proceeds be used for operating expenses or for any purpose other than acquisition, preservation, protection, or care of collections.

H. Disposal may be by exchange, donation, or public sale with scholarly or cultural organizations as the preferred recipients.

I. Materials deaccessioned shall not be privately sold, given, or otherwise transferred to the Corporation's staff or trustees.

This Policy was formally approved and adopted by the Board of Trustees of the (*name of Corporation*) _____
at a meeting held at (*location*) _____ on
(*Date*) _____.
Signed (officer): _____
Typed or printed name of officer: _____
Title: _____

Credit: Used with permission. "A Sample Collections Management Policy from the New York State Education Department's Museum Chartering Office website—for sample use only."

APPENDIX III

Media Alert: Boscobel House and Gardens

1601 Rte 9D ~ Garrison, New York 10524

MEDIA ALERT

More info:

Donna S. Blaney

dblaney@boscobel.org

FOR IMMEDIATE RELEASE

Boscobel House & Gardens
Donates Historic Painting to the West Point Museum

(Garrison, NY—March 2015)—By unanimous action of the Boscobel Board of Directors, a painting of West Point and the Hudson River has been deaccessioned at Boscobel and is being presented to the West Point Museum. The oil on canvas titled *View of West Point* dates to 1856, but is unsigned. The quality of the imagery and execution suggests it was painted by a highly competent, self-taught artist of the period. While many members of the Hudson River School are well known today, this picture by an unknown painter clearly illustrates the Hudson River's enduring appeal for artists. The Hudson Highlands, which appear in the background of the picture, were featured frequently and prominently in 19th-century prints, paintings, drawings, and eventually photography.

As with most museums, Boscobel periodically reviews its collections for relevancy, content, condition, and mission focus. The most recent such survey touched on a limited number of objects that were deemed inappropriate for the mission of the organization. The date of the *View of West Point* is well outside Boscobel's focus on the 1805–1820 Federal period of America's history. While the landscape falls outside of Boscobel's collecting interests, it is particularly appropriate for the West Point Museum. The United States Military Academy is nestled along the shoreline of the highlands and has long been a popular site with tourists and military personnel alike.

Speaking of the gift, Boscobel Executive Director Steven Miller noted, "We are pleased to donate the *View of West Point* to the West Point Museum. It will be preserved and remain in this area in a public collection and thus be appreciated for years to come."

Marlana L. Cook, curator of art at the West Point Museum, responds, "The West Point Museum is delighted to receive this wonderful painting into its collections. It is a lovely piece that will enhance our collection of Hudson River School paintings and help to educate the Cadets at the Military Academy about the history and landscape of West Point. We are grateful to our friends at Boscobel for donating this artwork to the West Point Museum."

Used with permission. Reprinted from Boscobel.org, 2017.

APPENDIX IV

Metropolitian Museum of Art Deaccessioning Policy

VI. Deaccessioning
A. General Principles

The term "deaccession" means that a work is removed from the collection and considered for disposal by sale, exchange, or other means. Any deaccession of a work should be solely for the advancement of the Museum's mission. The criteria for determining whether an object should be deaccessioned include, but are not limited to, the following:

1. The work does not further the mission of the Museum.
2. The work is redundant or is a duplicate and is not necessary for research or study purposes.
3. The work is of lesser quality than other objects of the same type in the collection or about to be acquired.
4. The work lacks sufficient aesthetic merit or art historical importance to warrant retention.
5. The Museum is ordered to return an object to its original and rightful owner by a court of law; the Museum determines that another entity is the rightful owner of the object; or the Museum determines that the return of the object is in the best interest of the Museum.
6. The Museum is unable to conserve the object in a responsible manner.
7. The work is unduly difficult or impossible to care for or store properly.

The Museum may deaccession but generally does not dispose of works determined to be forgeries. Curatorial departments generally retain these works for study purposes or seek the Director's permission to destroy the objects, unless it can be determined that disposal can be accomplished in a responsible manner without confusion to a possible buyer. Works incorrectly attributed or dated may be deaccessioned, provided that the new information or attribution is provided.

No Trustee, Officer, employee, volunteer, or family member of such individuals may purchase deaccessioned works of art directly from the Museum or at auction if consigned by the Museum.

All funds received from deaccessioned works shall be used to fund the purchase of other works.

B. Guidelines for Deaccessioning Gifts

The Museum shall honor all legal restrictions attaching to the gift or bequest of any work of art. In addition, donor requests which do not impose any legal obligation accompanying the bequest or gift of any work of art will be respected to the extent feasible, unless modified by the donor, or if the donor is not living, the donor's heirs or legal representatives. Before proceeding to recommend that a donated work be deaccessioned, the curator first reviews the records of gift to confirm that the gift is unrestricted.

In addition, no work acquired by the Museum through gift or bequest valued by the Museum at $50,000 or more will be disposed of within 25 years following its receipt if objected to, after appropriate notice, by the donor or the donor's heirs or representatives.

C. Procedures for Deaccessioning

The Board of Trustees approved detailed Procedures for Deaccessioning and Disposing of Works of Art at a Special Meeting held on June 20, 1973. The Procedures were updated in February 2005 and are available upon request from the Counsel's Office.

Excerpted from "Collections Management Policy" on the Metropolitan Museum of Art's website (https://www.metmuseum.org/about-the-met/ policies-and-documents/collections-managementpolicy), © 2015 by The Metropolitan Museum of Art, New York. Reprinted by permission.

APPENDIX V

Sample Deaccession List: Boscobel House and Gardens Deaccession List

Objects recommended for deaccession from the collection of Boscobel Restoration, Inc.:
Judith Pavelock, Curator and Collection Manager
October 15, 2014

1

F 76.21 (Tracy 67)
Object: Linen press
Place of origin: New York City
Date: 1785–1800
Materials: Mahogany, mahogany veneer, tulip poplar, white pine
Dimensions: 87½ x 55¼ x 24 inches
Source: Purchased from Earl V. Smith, Norfolk, CT, 8/13/76, who identified the case piece as the "Fulton-Ludlow Linen Press" without further documentation or comment. The Fulton Ludlow House was in Claverack, NY.
Status: Brewer Room Storage
Deaccession justification: Four other linen press/wardrobes remain in collection; this one is redundant and to be replaced with newly acquired Phyfe documented linen press (2014.01).
Recommendation: Auction

2

F 76.6 (Tracy 45)
Object: Urn stand

Place of origin: New York City
Date: 1810–1820 and later
Materials: Mahogany, cherry, tulip poplar, pine, marble, brass.
Dimensions: 29³/₄ x 17¹/₂ inches
Source: Bernard and S. Dean Levy, New York, NY, 1976
Status: Front drawing room
Deaccession justification: This stand does not relate to any known New York federal furnishings and may have been altered from another form.
Recommendation: Auction

3

2009.03
Object: Chest of drawers
Place of origin: New York City
Date: 1810–1820
Materials: Mahogany, tulip poplar, pine, brass
Dimensions: H: 49⁹/₁₆ x W: 48 x D: 23⁹/₁₆ inches
Source: Purchase, The Odell House, Hartsdale, NY, through the Sons of the American Revolution, Inc., Robert Stackpole 2009
Status: Gate house
Deaccession justification: Conservation/conditions issues are more than value—split in top, brasses not original; better examples of this form exist in collection.
Recommendation: Auction

4

F 77.13 (Tracy 58)
Object: Dressing table
Place of origin: New York City
Date: 1810–1820 and later
Materials: Mahogany, mahogany veneer, tulip poplar, white pine, brass
Dimensions: 64¹/₂ x 41 x 20¹/₂ inches
Source: Israel Sack, Inc., New York, NY, 5/13/77
Status: Dressing room
Deaccession justification: This dressing table appears to have been originally a common serving table that was enhanced by a later addition of small drawers, elliptic splashboard, and looking glass.

Recommendation: Auction

F 70.7
Object: Pembroke table
Place of origin: New England
Date: 1790–1825
Materials: Cherry, maple, white pine
Dimensions: 24 x 47 inches
Source: Purchase, William C. Kennedy 1970
Status: Gate house
Deaccession justification: Duplicate object; better examples exist in the
    collection.
Recommendation: Auction

6

F 60.1 (Tracy 2)
Object: Easy chair
Place of origin: Mid-Atlantic Region or Connecticut River Valley
Date: 1790–1815
Materials: Cherry, lightwood inlays, pine frame [NOT EXAMINED],
    wool moreen upholstery
Dimensions: 47 x 35 x 29 inches
Source: Ginsburg & Levy, New York, NY, 12/21/60
Status: Gatehouse
Deaccession justification: The chair is outside of the geographic scope; a
    better intact New York example (Boscobel accession 2009.01) replaced
    this chair in 2014.

*Used with permission. Deaccession list is from Collections files, Boscobel House
and Gardens.*

APPENDIX VI

The Metropolitan Museum of Art Press Release, June 26, 1973: "Metropolitian Museum Issues Trustee Report on Recent Disposals"

HOLD FOR RELEASE 6:00 P.M.
TUESDAY, JUNE 26, 1973

New York, NY 10028212 879 5500

Douglas Dillon, President of The Metropolitan Museum of Art, announced today that the Special Committee of Trustees headed by Roswell Gilpatric, which was appointed in March to review Museum disposal policies and procedures, has completed its report.

The Committee members are: Mrs. Vincent Astor, Mrs. Mary Lothrop Bundy, J. Richardson Dilworth, Robert M. Pennoyer–Secretary, Richard S. Perkins, Francis T. P. Plimpton, Charles B. Wrightsman, and Roswell Gilpatric–Chairman.

The 42-page document, titled *Report on Art Transaction 1971–1973*, which has been authorized for release by the Board of Trustees, together with certain modifications in the procedures for the disposal of works of art which have been approved by the Board, are being made public today, Mr. Dillon said.

The Special Committee was formed to examine the overall adequacy of existing procedures governing the disposal of works of art; to recommend changes in the procedures if necessary; and to review recent sales and exchanges which had been the subject of public comment in the press and elsewhere.

The Report's chief findings can be summarized as follows:

1. The policy and principle of continued refinement of the collections through judicious disposal and selective acquisition

was sustained as an integral and necessary function of the Museum.

2. With reference to existing procedures of checks and balances governing the deaccessioning and disposal of works of art, the Committee concluded that these procedures were properly applied and observed in the recent transactions that drew public attention. However, although the procedures were found to be sound and effective as safeguards, they apparently were inadequate in preventing doubts and misunderstanding in the public mind concerning art transactions and perhaps contributed to that misunderstanding.

3. Therefore, in accordance with a recommendation from the Committee, the Board of Trustees decided that, in response to mounting public interest, the Museum's policy should provide for the fullest practicable public disclosure.

4. Accordingly, the Committee recommended and the Board approved a number of modifications in the Museum's disposal procedures. In the broad scope these provide for greater public disclosure; take account of the interests and views of museums, scholars, and others outside the Metropolitan; increase protection for the interests of donors; and provide for notification to the Attorney General of intended transactions.

These modifications were drafted after consultation with the Attorney General of the State of New York.

They may be summarized as follows:

1. The Museum will, as in the past, consistently honor legal restrictions attaching to the gift or bequest of any work of art. In addition, requests which do not impose any legal obligation accompanying the bequest or gift of any work of art will be respected to the extent feasible, unless modified by the donor or, if the donor is not living, the donor's heirs or legal representatives, on notice to the Attorney General of the State of New York.

2. No work of art valued by the Museum at $10,000 or more will be disposed of within 25 years following its receipt if objected

to after appropriate notice, by the donor or the donor's heirs or legal representatives. This policy will apply to any work of art, including gifts or bequests which are not subject to any legal obligation or accompanied by any non-binding request.

3. No object, valued by the Museum at more than $25,000, which has been on exhibition in the Museum within the preceding ten years, will be disposed of until at least 45 days after the issue of a public notice identifying the work and giving the range of its estimated value based on outside appraisals. Copies of such notice will be available to museums, scholars, and art historians who request them. At the conclusion of this 45-day period, public comments will be studied, and either the Board or its Executive Committee will again consider the work in question and make the final decision.

4. All future sales of works of art for cash valued by the Museum at in excess of $5,000 will be at public auction, unless the proposed sale is to another museum or similar institution, in which case consideration will be given to requests for extended times of payment.

5. Whenever it is proposed that the Museum offer for exchange or sale to another museum, or for exchange to any third party, an object valued by the Museum at more than $25,000, at least three disinterested outside appraisals will be obtained. In setting up the procedures for selecting such outside appraisers, the Museum will solicit the views of knowledgeable third parties.

6. The Museum's Annual Report will include a statement of the cash proceeds from the sale of objects disposed of during the relevant year, and will describe each object sold or exchanged valued at more than $25,000. All reattributions of major works of art made during the preceding year will also be discussd in the Annual Report.

7. Promptly after action by the Board of Trustees, the Executive Committee or the Acquisitions Committee to deaccession any work of art with a Museum valuation in excess of $5,000, notice will be given to the Attorney General of the State of New York at least 15 days (unless otherwise agreed upon with

the Attorney General at the time) prior to the sale or exchange of such work of art, specifying the restrictions, if any, applicable to such work of art.

The numerous checks and balances that already exist in the Museum's disposal procedures, such as requirements for independent appraisals, and Trustee approval of all disposals, remain unchanged.

Roughly half of the Report is devoted to factual, detailed summaries of eight specific transactions involving paintings from the Museum's collections which took place between January 1971 and February 1973 and about which questions had been raised publicly. These transactions include two exchanges, four sales to dealers and two auction sales. A total of 201 paintings are involved, 3/4 of which were sold at public auction.

These are discussed in the contexts of both the Museum's Comprehensive Architectural Plan, and the purchase in November 1970 of the Velazquez *Juan de Pareja*. The Architectural Plan first initiated in 1967 placed a finite physical limit to future expansion and thereby limited future acquisitions as well. Almost every department was required to plan and control its growth. The general policy was to be one of upgrading holdings through careful disposal and selective acquisition. The disposal of paintings between 1971 and 1973 was a direct result of that policy.

In November 1970 after repeated attempts to interest other museums in the joint purchase of Velazquez's *Juan de Pareja* had failed, the Museum bought the painting alone, for the sum of $5,592,000. Except for $750,000 contributed by Trustees, the painting was paid for by an appropriation from the principal of the Fletcher Fund, a major fund restricted to use for art purchases. In order to avoid a permanent reduction of this size in the principal of the Fletcher Fund, the Trustees decided to reimburse it over a period of time to the extent of $2,000,000. One of the means subsequently employed to carry out this decision was the disposal of a number of paintings, almost all of which would have been disposed of eventually under the overall plan of refining the collections.

The Trustees in approving the modified procedures reemphasized their approval of the policy that the Museum continue to pursue possibilities for the joint purchase of major works of art with other institutions.

The Report briefly reviews the history of the deaccessioning and disposal of works of art at the Metropolitan since 1885, explaining the origins of the practice and citing its first formulation as official policy under an 1887 Trustee Resolution. Described in some detail are an 1885 sale of duplicate Cypriote material; two auction sales (the first in the Museum's history) held in 1928; the sale in 1929 of 159 paintings and 675 other works of art which had accumulated, the Trustees then noted, from over 50 years of acquisition; the 1956 and 1957 disposals of 8,130 works of decorative art including 340 paintings, sold because they were "inferior to other examples owned by the Museum" and "no longer desirable for exhibition or study purposes."

Instances of noteworthy acquisitions made through exchange with both private dealers and other museums prior to 1971 are also described.

Also discussed are the two public auctions of coins in 1972 and 1973; the circumstances surrounding the deaccessioning of the *Odalisque* which had been attributed to Ingres, and the later decision to retain it; the Museum's position in disposing of part of the collection left to the Museum by Miss Adelaide Milton de Groot and figure policy for handling this collection; and finally the purchase of the Calyx Krater in 1972, in which the Committee found that the Museum had taken appropriate precautions to ensure that all applicable laws, here and abroad, were observed.

With regard to the krater, recently in early May, it was reported from Rome that Italian authorities had come into possession of some fragments which they attributed to Euphronios and which they felt might be linked to the Museum's krater. There are no missing pieces in the Museum's krater that could match those which have been described. The Museum has officially invited the Italian authorities to come to New York, bring these fragments with them, and conduct a personal inspection of the krater. The Museum is confident that such an inspection would confirm that the fragments, if they are by Euphronios, come from another krater, not the one in the Museum.

The disposition of every painting deaccessioned between January 1971 and June 1973 is accounted for in an appendix. This information together with facts contained in the text of the Report fully document appraisals, curatorial valuations, dates of deaccessioning and reaccessioning, sale proceeds received, and the use of funds realized from disposals.

On balance, the Committee felt that the results of the Museum's policies have been in the best interests of the institution and the public it serves. The most convincing evidence that the collections have been enriched is available in the galleries, where such works as the *Juan de Pareja*, the Euphronios Krater, Carracci's *Coronation of the Virgin*, David Smith's *Becca* and other works of art testify to the continuing improvement and refinement of the collections.

(END)

FOR FURTHER INFORMATION please contact Jack Frizzelle, Department of Public Information, The Metropolitan Museum of Art, 82nd Street and Fifth Avenue, New York, NY 10028.

Tel: (212) 879-5500.

Credit: Used with permission of The Metropolitan Museum of Art.

INDEX

Page references for figures are italicized

ABOUT THE AUTHOR

Steven Miller has devoted nearly fifty years to museum service. He has been a curator, midlevel administrator, director, educator, trustee, writer, and consultant. His career began with the Museum of the City of New York in its curatorial department for paintings, prints, and photographs. He concluded that job as senior curator. He was then the assistant director of the Maine State Museum; director of museums at the Western Reserve Historical Society, Cleveland, Ohio; executive director of the Bennington Museum, Bennington, Vermont; executive director of the Morris Museum, Morristown, New Jersey; and executive director of Boscobel Restoration, Garrison, New York.

Miller has long supported museum profession organizations. He does site visits for the accreditation program of the American Alliance of Museums. He is currently on the board of the Greater Hudson Heritage Network; the Bard College Alumni Board of Governors; and Historic Huguenot Street, New Paltz, New York. Miller received a BA in sculpture from Bard College and an international graduate certificate in the Principals of Conservation Science at the International Centre for the Study of the Preservation and the Restoration of Cultural Property (ICCROM) in Rome, Italy.

Miller has written, lectured, consulted, and been closely involved in deaccessioning matters since the practice started receiving widespread attention in the mid-1970s. He has two adult children and lives in new Hope, Pennsylvania, with his wife, Jane, a fund-raiser with the Nature Conservancy.